THE REAL

CHILI

COOKBOOK

THE REAL
CHILI
COOKBOOK

AMERICA'S 100 ALL-TIME
FAVORITE RECIPES

MARJIE LAMBERT

CHARTWELL
BOOKS, INC.

A QUINTET BOOK

Published by Chartwell Books
A Division of Book Sales, Inc.
114 Northfield Avenue
Edison, New Jersey 08837

First paperback edition published 1997.

ISBN 0-7858-0802-7

CREATIVE DIRECTOR: *Richard Dewing*
DESIGNER: *Simon Balley*
SENIOR EDITOR: *Laura Sandelson*
EDITOR: *Caroline Ball*
PHOTOGRAPHER: *David Armstrong*

Typeset in Great Britain by
Central Southern Typesetters, Eastbourne
Manufactured in Malaysia by
C.H. Colour Scan SDN BHD
Printed in Singapore by
Star Standard Industries (Pte) Ltd

AUTHOR ACKNOWLEDGMENTS

With thanks to Terry, who hopes he never smells cumin again, to Laura at Quintet;
and to my colleagues at the *Sun Sentinel*, who boldly tasted what no one had tasted before.

Contents

Introduction

The history of chili has as many twists and tangents as a tale by a champion story-teller. And like any tall tale, it is impossible to sort out the facts, exaggerations, embroidered truths, competing claims, and downright lies about chili. Who made the first pot of chili, and when? There are stories of meat-and-chile stews dating to the 16th century, and there were probably 16th century men who bragged of eating chili so hot that a week later, their breath could still boil water. But it wasn't until well into the 19th century that chili became institutionalized, a staple of the American frontier. Why? It was a hardy food of non-perishable ingredients that were easily transported, a simple concoction of wild chiles, animal fat, and dried beef or hunter's game. Long hours of simmering softened the toughest, driest meats, and the chiles disguised any rancid flavor.

Lavanderas, *Mexican laundresses who followed the Mexican Army across the Rio Grande and later served Texas and U.S. militiamen, simmered the tough, stringy meat of the scrawny cattle and deer that grazed along the U.S./Mexican border. Chuckwagon cooks boiled scraps of meat and fat with chiles, onions, and oregano from the "spice groves" that they planted along the cattle trails. Frontiersmen and gold miners* stuffed their saddlebags with jerky that had been pounded with fat and chiles, then boiled the dried meat to make a spicy dinner. And the chili queens of San Antonio sold bowls of chili from their stalls in the city's Military Plaza.

None of those unappetizing beginnings would have predicted success. Given chili's history, it is amazing it survived into the age of refrigeration, when dried meat and harsh spices were no longer necessities. But instead of fading into obscurity with hardtack and other disagreeable foods, chili changed with the times. Cooks used fresh, albeit tough cuts of meat. Buffalo and venison chili became more commonplace, replaced later by beef and pork. When meat was scarce or expensive, they stretched it by adding beans or brown rice to chili. Canary Islanders who immigrated to Texas brought cumin with them, adding a distinctive flavor that is mandatory among most chili lovers.

By the late 1800s, chili was being canned. The San Antonio Chili Stand – which began with that city's chili queens – was a feature of the 1893 World's Fair in Chicago. But chili's popularity really didn't spread outside Texas until the early part of the 20th century. It peaked during the Depression when a bowl of chili with crackers was one of the heartiest

Cindy Reed, proud winner of the chili cookoff in Houston, 1992 and 1993. (Picture courtesy Chili Appreciation Society International)

and cheapest meals available in diners. Then World War II brought rationing, and chili disappeared from many menus.

Its popularity did not revive until the 1960s, when President Lyndon B. Johnson's passion for Pedernales River Chili – made with venison and tomatoes – was widely publicized. Suddenly, chili's popularity exploded.

Today, chili is one of America's most popular dishes. In 1977, chili was named the official State Dish of Texas, and a contingent of chiliheads regularly lobbies for it to be named the official dish of the United States. Chili has been influenced by Mexican cooking but it is an all-American dish. The Chili Appreciation Society International and a splinter group, the International Chili Society, hold frequent chili cookoffs that draw tens of thousands of people. There is now a chili cookoff circuit, much like the beauty pageant circuit, where cooks compete in smaller contests to win the right to compete in the big ones.

What began as a simple dish has assumed almost mythical status, boosted by beer, bragging, and the cook's secret ingredient, a combination that is present almost anywhere chili is simmering on the fire.

What is chili? In its purest form, the ingredients are the same that chuckwagon cooks stirred into frontier-era chili – meat, chiles, onions, and spices – although the meat is fresher, and cooks use less fat today. Variety comes from the different cuts of meat and combinations of chiles and spices used. But few people outside Texas make such a basic chili. Even in Texas, many cooks use a little tomato sauce for color and body. Others use masa harina, flour, or cracker meal to thicken chili. For cooks who stray beyond basic chili, beer, lime juice, chopped tomatoes, celery, bell peppers, and a pinch of sugar are common additions. Chiliheads will argue endlessly over whether fresh minced garlic is superior to garlic powder, or whether mild New Mexico chile powder is superior to California chile powder.

Beyond those basics, chili's bold flavors invite creativity. Every passionate chili cook has a secret ingredient or two. Maybe it is an exotic chile or chili powder. Often, however, it is something truly unexpected that adds a mystery note to the symphony of flavors: unsweetened cocoa, coffee, allspice, turmeric, caraway seeds, tequila, corn, olives, finely chopped sun-dried tomatoes, mole powder, and roasted garlic are ingredients that show up in a surprising number of chili pots.

And that doesn't even take into account vegetarian chili – a spicy vegetable stew that most chiliheads won't recognize.

So what's the perfect chili recipe? It's all a matter of taste – and what ingredients you have on hand when an urgent craving for chili strikes. The recipes offered in these pages provide enough variety to suit any mood, any budget, any pantry, and any palate, from the delicate to the asbestos. But don't limit yourself. If none of these chili recipes suits your mood or your taste, change them. That's the final ingredient of a great chili: Creativity.

1

INGREDIENTS AND TECHNIQUES

If you avoid discussions of religion and politics because of the arguments they provoke, stay away from the subject of chili too. Debates about chili are fierce, emotional, and highly personal. They often make political or religious arguments sound tame. With or without beans? Kidney suet or canola oil? How coarsely should meat be ground? And are you a sissy if you don't like habanero chiles? Chiliheads believe there is only one true chili – theirs. And they are not likely to reveal the secret ingredient or technique that makes their chili superior to all others. But if there was really only one true chili, there would be no need for chili cookoffs and chili cookbooks, and no grounds for bragging. And what fun is chili-making without bragging? Following is a listing of common and some uncommon chili ingredients. Some may violate the purity standards of old-line chiliheads, but if you wanted purity, you could passively follow their recipe instead of following your heart – and your palate.

CHILES

The chile – fresh, dried, or ground into powder – is the soul of the stew we call chili.

Chiles – *capsicum* – are native to the Americas and especially to Mexico. Christopher Columbus brought the chile back from the New World. Now more than 200 varieties grow around the world, and all chiliheads have their favorites. The jalapeño is the most widely available chile in the United States, but a chilihead is likely to scoff at the ordinariness of the jalapeño, favoring a serrano, a habanero, or a Thai bird's eye chile instead. An amateur may brag about how hot he likes his chiles, but a true chilihead will talk about the underlying flavors – the earthy, slightly chocolate flavor of the poblano, the hot-sweet intensity of a cayenne, the nuttiness of a dried cascabel.

Today's cooks have many choices of chiles, which come primarily in three forms: fresh, dried, and powdered. Chile paste is hard to find outside of specialty stores and mail-order sources, but can be used in place of soaked and puréed dried chiles. Canned chiles are also available, but – except for the chipotle chile and pickled jalapeños (*en escabeche*) – are inferior to other chile products.

ANAHEIM The Anaheim, also called the California chile, is the mildest member of the chile family and a cousin of the New Mexico chile. It is widely available fresh, probably second to the jalapeño, and is often canned and labelled simply "green chilies." It is pale green, smooth, 5 to 7 inches long and 1 inch or so wide. Dried, it is a deep burgundy color and is one of the most readily available dried chiles. A mild California chile powder is made from the Anaheim. In chilis, the Anaheim in any form is usually used in combination with hotter chiles.

ANCHO See poblano.

ARBOL The chile de arbol is narrow, about 3 inches long, and bright orange-red. It is very hot. It is most often found dried – sometimes labelled only "dried red chiles" – although other small, hot, dried red chiles such as serranos may also be labelled as chiles de arbol. Pure chile de arbol powder may be found in the Mexican section of some very well-stocked grocery stores.

CALIFORNIA See Anaheim.

CAYENNE The cayenne is bright red, thin, and pointed, 3 to 7 inches long. It is extremely hot, yet sweet, with a flavor similar to Thai bird's eye chiles, and is an ingredient in Asian as well as Mexican dishes. It is most familiar dried and ground into cayenne pepper – also called simply red pepper – which will add heat but not much flavor to any dish.

CHIPOTLE See Jalapeño.

HABANERO One of the two hottest chiles in the world, the habanero – its name means from Havana – is most widely used in the Yucatan, but has recently gained popularity among maso-chistic chiliheads in the U.S. The habanero is lantern shaped and looks like a miniature bell pepper, just 2 inches high. Its color ranges from green to bright orange. It is related to the Scotch Bonnet, an equally hot chile from the Caribbean. Fresh habaneros are showing up in a growing number of well-stocked grocery stores, especially those in Hispanic or Caribbean neighborhoods. Habanero chile powder and crushed dried habaneros are scarce but can be found.

Anaheim

Ancho

Arbol

Dried Habanero

Fresh Habanero

JALAPEÑO The jalapeño, the most widely available fresh chile in the U.S., is hot, although there are many varieties of chile that are hotter. Jalapeños are usually 2 to 3 inches long, smooth, glossy, and taper to a rounded end. Although most are sold green, they will turn bright red if left on the bush to ripen. Several raw, chopped, and unseeded jalapeños added to chili will turn up the heat considerably. Roasting jalapeños gives them a marvelous flavor, but they do not need to be roasted. Dried jalapeños are quite scarce. Jalapeño chile powder is also hard to find. Smoked jalapeños, called *chipotles*, have a wonderful, not at all subtle, smoky flavor and are a delicious addition to chili. They do not lose any of their heat in the smoking process. Chipotles are available canned in adobo sauce, and can occasionally, be found dried. Tart, pickled jalapeños, called *jalapeños in escabeche*, are more often used as a garnish than an ingredient.

NEGRO See pasilla.

NEW MEXICO This is the chile that Southwesterners rhapsodize about. The New Mexico chile is a

relative of the Anaheim and resembles it in size and shape, but inspires far more passion than its Californian cousin. Don't ever suggest to a chilihead that the Anaheim is in the same league as the beloved New Mexico chile! It is a light to medium green that darkens to a deep red if left on the bush to ripen. New Mexico green chiles are usually used fresh: the reds are usually dried or roasted and frozen, but it is possible to find fresh New Mexico reds and dried New Mexico greens. In general, the green chile ranges in heat from moderate to hot; the red is hot. New Mexico chile powders are also popular.

PASILLA Also called the *chile negro*, the pasilla is very dark, purple-black in color. It is long and slim like the Anaheim, but has wrinkled skin. The flavor is intense and moderately spicy, with just a bit more heat and none of the sweetness of the poblano. It is more readily available dried than fresh. It is often used in commercial chili powder blends. The dried poblano is sometimes mislabelled as pasilla. Held up to the light, a dried poblano (called an *ancho*) is reddish, while the pasilla is brown-black.

POBLANO Although only a moderately spicy chile, the poblano has a complex, earthy flavor with hints of chocolate. Green chile stews are usually made with poblanos, which can be used in the large quantities required without making the stew scorchingly hot. In a hot chili, poblanos are used in combination with hotter chiles. It is almost always roasted and peeled. Strips of roasted poblanos, called rajas, make delicious garnishes for chili. In its dried form, the poblano is called *ancho*, although it is sometimes mislabelled as pasilla. The ancho has a rich chile flavor with hints of raisin, and adds a wonderful note to chilis.

SCOTCH BONNET The incendiary Scotch bonnet is a relative of the habanero and is often confused with its equally fiery cousin. The Scotch bonnet looks like a tiny tam-o'-shanter in colors of green, yellow, orange, and red. It is not widely available in the U.S., but a diligent search may find it in a grocery in a West Indian neighborhood.

SERRANO Small – about 2 inches long – and thin, the serrano is hotter than the jalapeño but not as hot as the cayenne or habanero. It is usually sold when glossy green, but it turns red if left on the bush.

Chipotle

Jalapeño

Scotch Bonnet

New Mexico

MISCELLANEOUS CHILE ITEMS

CHILI POWDER Chili powder is a mix of spices that usually includes pure chile powder, cumin, oregano, and garlic powder, but each manufacturer's blend is different. Typically ancho or pasilla chile powder is used to produce a mild blend. Chili powder provides an underlying chile flavor but does not provide heat. It is usually used in combination with cayenne, Tabasco sauce, crushed chile flakes, or a pure hot chile powder when a hot chili is desired. Some spice companies also produce a hotter blend, called hot or Mexican chili powder, made with hotter chile powder. This will add moderate heat to a dish. Chile molido means pure, unspiced chile powder.

CHILE FLAKES Also called chile caribe, these are dried, crushed red chiles, usually New Mexico chiles, and are almost always very hot.

TABASCO SAUCE Tabasco sauce is a hot-pepper sauce made from the fermented Tabasco chile, vinegar, and salt. The Tabasco chile, from the Mexican state of Tabasco, is a cousin of the cayenne. It is a small, red fiery chile that is not available commercially. Tabasco sauce has been produced since before the Civil War, but as chiles and spicy foods have grown in popularity, Tabasco has had competition from a great variety of hot pepper sauces.

▲ *A range of store cupboard ingredients that any serious chili cook should keep.*

SAFETY PRECAUTIONS FOR COOKING WITH CHILES

Chiles' capsaicin content makes them difficult to work with. The capsaicin not only provides the heat on your palate, it will also make your lips, your fingers, your face sting if you get it on your skin. Because capsaicin is not water-soluble, rinsing your skin with water will not decrease the burn and may spread it. If the sting is in your mouth, a dairy product – milk, sour cream, yogurt – or a starchy food such as bread, rice, or beans will help. If it is on your hands or face, soap will help a little; rubbing a little shortening on the area, then washing it off with soap may also help.

Prevention is better, though. Wear latex gloves, the more snug, the better. My sister-in-law, a nurse, gave me some of her surgical gloves – I like them better than other gloves because they are very thin and snug. In a pinch, protect your hand by putting it in a plastic bag before you handle chiles.

Remember that the irritating chile oils get on knives, work surfaces and dish rags, and that rinsing with water will not get rid of the capsaicin. The items must be washed thoroughly with soap, preferably in the dishwasher.

Never touch your eyes when you are working with chiles. The burning sensation on your fingers is minimal compared to the pain it will cause in your eyes.

Although roasting the chiles will mellow their heat slightly, they still contain capsaicin, which will burn your fingers. Protect your hands when working with roasted chiles, just as you would with raw chiles.

ROASTING CHILES

Roasting chiles gives them a wonderful flavor and takes the edge off their heat. It also allows easy removal of the tough skin on some larger chiles such as Anaheims and poblanos. Smaller chiles, including habanero, serrano, and jalapeño, do not need to have their thin skins removed, but may be roasted for the flavor.

Chiles can be roasted whole in the broiler and turned (using tongs) during cooking, or cut into two or three large, flat pieces that do not need to be turned. Place the pieces skin side up. The chiles should be 4 to 6 inches below the broiler.

Watch them carefully as they cook. They are ready when the skin is blistered and mostly blackened. They will not cook evenly. If you wait for the skin to be solidly blackened, the flesh may be partly scorched and ruined.

As you remove chiles from the broiler, place them in a plastic or paper bag, a covered heat-proof bowl or, if you are only roasting one or two chiles, in a foil pouch. Seal the bag or pouch, or put the cover on the bowl. The chiles will steam as they cool, which will make it easy to remove the skins. Leave the chiles for at least 10 minutes. Then peel off the skins. If working with whole chiles, remove the stems and seeds. Remember to wear plastic gloves to protect your hands from chile juices.

STEP 1

Remove freshly roasted chiles from the broiler

STEP 2

Place chiles in a plastic bag to cool

STEP 3

Peel off the skins

COOKING WITH DRIED CHILES

In some markets, as many or more chiles are available in their dried form than are available fresh or powdered. Dried chiles can be turned into chile powder or chile purée.

To make chile powder, lightly toast the chiles in the oven. Use an ungreased baking sheet and set the oven at 400°F. Toast them a few minutes, until they are somewhat brittle and give off a chile fragrance. Do not allow them to darken – they will have a burned flavor that will ruin them. Let the toasted chiles cool. Remove the stems and seeds, cut or break them into pieces, and grind them in a food processor or spice grinder.

To make a purée, remove the stems and seeds and cut the chiles into two to four pieces. Put them in a deep, narrow heat-proof bowl. Pour just enough boiling water over them to cover. Stir to be sure all pieces are covered. Let the chiles soak 30 minutes. Pour the chiles and their soaking liquid into a blender or food processor. Purée until smooth. Strain to remove seeds and bits of skin, discard the solids. Use the strained sauce in cooking. The chiles also may be simmered in water, beer, or beef or chicken stock, then puréed.

MEAT

Frontier-era chilis were made with beef jerky, buffalo, or venison. The vast majority of chilis today use beef or pork or a combination. One of chili's charms is that the toughest, cheapest cuts of meat turn into tender morsels by the time a pot of chili has simmered for an hour or so. Don't waste your money on tender steaks, chops, or roasts. Beef chuck, pork shoulder, tri-tip, flank steak, round steak, and pork loin — all trimmed of excess fat — are good chili cuts. Venison, although not commonly stocked in most grocery stores, remains a favorite.

Ideally, your butcher or grocer sells a coarse grind of meat called chili grind. It is coarser than hamburger, but finer than meat cut into small cubes. If you have a meat grinder, you can grind your own meat at home. An imperfect alternative is the food processor, which has an unfortunate tendency to produce an uneven mix of meat so finely ground that it has been turned to mush, and big chunks of meat that need to be chopped by hand. Throw a few 2-inch chunks of meat at a time into the food processor and use the pulse switch to grind the meat in very short bursts. Adding chunks of onion at the beginning helps. Otherwise, use hamburger or hand cut the meat into ¼-inch to ½-inch dice.

FAT

Historically, chili was cooked with a lot of fat — usually kidney suet, salt pork, lard, or bacon drippings, all of which add more flavor than vegetable oil. And that is in addition to whatever fat was in the meat, which was sometimes a lot. Some say chili eaters began crumbling saltines into their chili because the crackers absorbed the grease that floated on top. Most of us have reduced the amount and type of fat we eat, and the most flavorful animal fats, like kidney suet, have fallen out of favor. Chili can be made with a relatively small amount of fat — minimal amounts can be used to brown meat and onions. Most recipes in this cookbook call for vegetable oil, but equal amounts of other fats can be substituted.

BEANS

The International Chili Society forbids the inclusion of beans in recipes entered in its cookoffs. But whether an ingredient in chili or cooked separately and served on the side, beans are a natural mate for chili. They provide a pleasant contrast in texture and flavor, and for the economical, help stretch a little meat a long way. Whenever possible, start with dried beans and soak and slow-cook them, especially when they are the primary ingredient in chili. Canned beans tend to have a mushier texture, and a less distinct flavor.

HERBS AND SPICES

CILANTRO Cilantro, also known as coriander or Chinese parsley, is a pungent herb with a distinctive taste that its detractors call soapy. Ubiquitous in Southwestern dishes, it is not as common in chilis. It is best added in the last few minutes of cooking. Dried cilantro lacks the flavor of fresh and is rarely used. Ground coriander seed is not a substitute for fresh cilantro, but is sometimes added to chilis for its own flavor.

CUMIN Cumin is what gives chili its distinctive flavor. This musky seasoning is usually used as a ground spice; however, chili connisseurs toast the whole cumin seed in a small, dry skillet, then grind it before adding to chili. Toasting the seed enhances the flavor.

GARLIC Garlic, one of nature's greatest gifts to the cook, is one of the staples of a chili-lover's pantry. Chili cooks often substitute garlic powder in competitions, where judges may deduct points for visible vegetables. If you are not entering your chili in a cookoff, add lots of fresh garlic.

OREGANO With chile powder and cumin, oregano is a basic chili seasoning. Use dried, not ground, oregano, and look for Mexican oregano, which has a sharper taste than European oreganos. If toasting and grinding whole cumin seeds, add the oregano to the skillet with the cumin for extra flavor.

◄ Tortilla chips, sour cream, chopped onion, grated cheese, and salsas are among the most popular chili garnishes.

GARNISHES

Some say it ruins perfectly good chili, but many people say a bowl of chili is incomplete without grated cheese sprinkled over the top. Others crumble handfuls of saltines into their chili. But this is a more respectful debate than whether beans belong in chili because, by definition, the garnishes are added by each individual to suit their taste, rather than imposed on them by a bullying cook.

Grated Cheddar or Monterey jack cheese and chopped white or yellow onions are the most common garnishes. But without getting into the ridiculous, chili is complemented by a large array of garnishes.

AVOCADOS Some people swear by them. I find their subtle flavor is overwhelmed by chili. If you insist on topping your chili with avocados, use the black-skinned Hass, which has more flavor than the smooth, green-skinned Fuerte.

CHEESE Grated Cheddar is the most popular, followed by Monterey jack. Feta and goat cheeses, with their assertive flavors, are an unexpected treat with chili. Queso anejo is a sharp Mexican cheese that goes well.

CHILES Just in case your chili doesn't have enough chile flavor, garnish it with chopped or sliced fresh jalapeños. *Rajas*, strips of roasted (and sometimes fried) poblano chiles, are good. Hardcore chiliheads float tiny dried red hot chiles, such as chilipiquins, on top of their chili, but this is more for looks than taste. The chilipiquins are rarely eaten, and care is taken that they are not broken and their fiery seeds spilled into the chili.

CHIPS Crumbled corn or tortilla chips add crunch and a salty flavor to chili.

CILANTRO Sprinkle chopped fresh cilantro over a bowl of chili rather than cooking it in the chili.

OLIVES Sliced black olives stand up surprisingly well to a spicy chili.

ONIONS Bowls of chopped white or yellow onions are traditionally served with chili, but red and green onions are also good.

SALTINES Crumbled over the top of chili, these crackers add crunch and help sop up grease.

SOUR CREAM This adds a tangy flavor to chili and takes the edge off fiery heat.

TORTILLAS Many chilis are delicious wrapped in warm corn or flour tortillas.

CHILI FOR PURISTS

The original chilis of Texas and the American Southwest were little more than tough or dried meat boiled with chili powders and other spices. Later, cooks added onion, garlic, and tomato, but for some purists, even those ingredients were frowned on. For them, the addition of beans was sacrilege – although they often served beans on the side. For them, we offer the following 32 chili recipes. They range from mild to smoke-coming-out-your-ears hot. Most use beef or pork, but some use venison, chicken, or turkey. None of them includes beans.

Double Pork Ancho-Chipotle Chili

MAKES 6 SERVINGS

This chili, made with cubed pork and pork sausage, has a thick, rich sauce. It is hot but not fiery. Big, meaty ancho chiles – dried poblanos – add a strong chile taste that is not overpowered by the heat.

ingredients

- 8 ounces pork sausage
- 2 pounds pork, cubed
- 2 Tbsp. vegetable oil
- 1½ medium onions, chopped
- 1 stalk celery, finely chopped
- ½ green bell pepper, finely chopped
- 3 cloves garlic, minced
- 8-ounce can tomato sauce
- 2 cups beef stock
- 4 ancho chiles
- 2 chipotle chiles, dried or canned
- 2 Tbsp. commercial chili powder
- 2 tsp. ground cumin
- 2 tsp. dried oregano
- 1 tsp. celery salt
- ½ tsp. sugar
- 1 Tbsp. lime juice
- 1–2 tsp. salt

● Crumble the sausage into a large skillet and cook until a little fat is rendered. Add the cubed pork and cook until the meat is browned. Remove the meat and discard any fatty cooking juices. Heat the oil and sauté the onion, celery, bell pepper, and garlic 5 minutes. Put the meat and vegetables in a large pot with the tomato sauce and beef stock. Bring to a boil, reduce heat and simmer.

● Cut the ancho chiles in half and remove the stems and seeds. If using dried chipotles, remove the stems. Put the dried chiles in a small, heat-proof bowl and pour 1 cup boiling water over them. Be sure all parts of the chiles are covered. Let the chiles sit in the hot water for 30 minutes. After soaking, put the chiles and their soaking water in a blender or food processor. If using canned chipotles, add them to the ancho chiles. Purée the chiles until a thick red sauce forms. Strain to remove seeds and bits of skin. Add the sauce to the chili along with the remaining ingredients, except salt.

● When the meat has simmered at least 1½ hours, add salt, taste, and adjust seasonings.

Beef Chili with Beer and Three Chiles

MAKES 4 SERVINGS

This is a traditional chili of beef in a hot, velvety sauce of mild Anaheim chiles, hot New Mexico chiles, and smoky chipotle chiles. Serve it with plain white rice to soak up the sauce.

- Split the dried chiles in half and remove the stems and seeds. (If using canned chipotles, do not add them at this point.) Put them in a small saucepan with the beer. Bring to a boil, reduce heat and simmer 30 minutes, stirring occasionally to be sure all parts of the chiles are softening.

- While the chiles are cooking, heat 1 tablespoon of the oil in a skillet or large pot and sauté the onions 5 minutes, then add the garlic and sauté 1 minute longer. Remove the onions from the pan. Heat the remaining 1 tablespoon oil and cook the beef, stirring frequently, until the beef is lightly browned on all sides. Put the beef and onions in a pot with the beef broth. Boil, reduce heat and simmer.

- Put the chiles and cooking liquid in a blender or food processor. If using canned chipotle chiles, remove the stems and put the chipotles in the blender or food processor. Purée until a thick red sauce forms. Strain the sauce to remove the bits of skin, then add the sauce to the meat. Stir in the seasonings and sugar. Continue to simmer at least 1 hour, until the meat is tender, adding beer, beef broth, or water if needed. Add salt, adjust seasonings to taste.

ingredients

- **2 dried Anaheim chiles**
- **2 dried New Mexico chiles**
- **2 chipotle chiles, dried or canned**
- **12-ounce bottle beer**
- **2 Tbsp. vegetable oil**
- **1 medium onion, chopped**
- **2 cloves garlic, minced**
- **2 pounds beef chuck, trimmed and cubed**
- **1 cup beef broth**
- **1 tsp. ground cumin**
- **1 tsp. paprika**
- **1 tsp. dried oregano**
- **½ tsp. sugar**
- **about 1 tsp. salt**

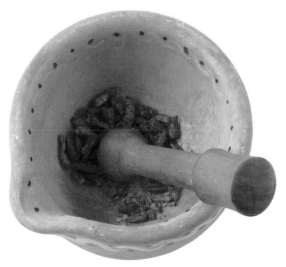

Rapid Fire Chili

MAKES 4 TO 5 SERVINGS

ingredients

2 dried New Mexico chiles

2 dried Anaheim chiles

2 pounds ground beef

1 Tbsp. vegetable oil

1 medium onion, chopped

8-ounce can tomato sauce

2 beef bouillon cubes

1 tsp. garlic powder

1 tsp. paprika

¼–½ tsp. cayenne

1 tsp. dried oregano

½ tsp. ground coriander seed

½ tsp. salt

● Cut the dried chiles in half and remove the stems and seeds. Put the chiles in a small, heat-proof bowl and pour 1 cup boiling water over them. Stir to be sure all parts of the chiles are covered with water. Let the chiles soak for 30 minutes. Put the chiles and soaking water in a blender or food processor and purée until a smooth sauce forms. Strain sauce.

● While the chiles are soaking, brown the beef in a large skillet. Remove the beef with a slotted spoon. Drain and discard the fat. Heat the oil and sauté the onion 5 minutes. Put the meat and onion in a large saucepan with the tomato sauce. Dissolve the bouillon cubes in 1 cup boiling water and add to the meat.

● Bring to a boil, reduce heat and simmer. Add the chile sauce as soon as it is ready. Add the remaining ingredients, except salt. The chili should simmer at least 20 minutes. Add a little water if needed while it is cooking. Add salt, taste, and adjust seasonings.

Boilermaker Chili

MAKES 4 SERVINGS

ingredients

3 dried Anaheim chiles

2 dried New Mexico chiles

3 Tbsp. vegetable oil

2 pounds cubed pork or beef

1 large onion, chopped

½ green bell pepper, chopped

1 stalk celery, chopped

2 cloves garlic, minced

8 ounces tomato sauce

12-ounce bottle beer

3 Tbsp. whiskey

2 tsp. ground cumin

1 tsp. paprika

1 tsp. dried oregano

½ tsp. black pepper

about 1 tsp. salt

● Split the dried chiles in half and remove the stems and seeds. Put the chiles in a small, heat-proof bowl and pour 1 cup boiling water over them. Let the chiles soak 30 minutes, stirring occasionally to make sure all parts of the chiles are covered with water.

● Heat 1 tablespoon of the oil in a skillet and cook the meat, turning occasionally, until all sides are lightly browned. Remove the meat from the skillet and set aside. Discard the fat in the skillet. Heat the remaining 2 tablespoons oil and sauté the onion, green pepper, celery, and garlic 5 minutes. Put the meat and sautéed vegetables in a large pot with the tomato sauce, beer, 2 tablespoons of the whiskey, and seasonings. Bring to a boil, reduce heat and simmer.

● Put the chiles and their soaking liquid in a blender or food processor. Purée until a smooth sauce forms. Strain to remove seeds and bits of skin and discard solids. Add the sauce to the chili. Continue simmering the chili, so the total simmering time is at least 1½ hours. Add salt and the remaining 1 tablespoon whiskey. Taste and adjust seasonings.

▼ *Boilermaker Chili*

Pork Chili with Smoked Paprika

MAKES 4 SERVINGS

This chili is only mildly spicy, but the pungent flavor is rounded out by the addition of smoked paprika.

ingredients

1 Tbsp. vegetable oil

2 pounds pork, cubed

1½ onions, chopped

1 stalk celery, finely chopped

3 cups chicken broth

8-ounce can tomato sauce

2 tsp. smoked paprika

1 Tbsp. commercial chili powder

1 tsp. dried oregano

about 1 tsp. salt

● Heat the oil in a large, deep skillet or pot and cook the pork until lightly browned on all sides. Add the onion and celery and cook 5 minutes.

● Add the remaining ingredients, except salt. Bring to a boil, reduce heat and simmer 1½ to 2 hours, adding water if needed. Add salt to taste.

▶ *Pork Chili with Smoked Paprika*

Jon's Stout Stuff Chili

MAKES 8 TO 10 SERVINGS

Jon Engellenner is a connoisseur of beer. So much so that he brews his own. One of his hobbies is cooking with beer, and this chili is a product of that. This is not a hot chili, "just stout stuff," Jon says. In his words, this chili "is complex, despite the simple recipe, and satisfying in small servings. Rather than searing its way through the taste buds, it melts across the palate like a hearty stew. It has the dense, chewable flavor of a patiently concocted gravy." Jon uses his own, home-brewed stout, but says any other will do.

ingredients

oil for frying

3½ pounds chuck steak, cut into small cubes

1 pound ground chuck

2 large onions, diced

1 large green Anaheim chile, diced

2 × 26-ounce bottles Stout

2 tsp. hot New Mexico chile powder

2 Tbsp. salt

28-ounce can tomato sauce

28-ounce can tomatoes

1 tsp. ground cumin

1 tsp. paprika

2 tsp. dried oregano

2–4 Tbsp. masa harina or flour

● In a big pot, heat a small amount of oil and brown the beef. Add the onions and green chile and brown. Reduce the heat and add all the other ingredients, except the masa harina or flour. Cook at "high simmer" 4 hours, stirring occasionally. Add the masa or flour dissolved in a little cold water to thicken.

Fiery Scotch Bonnet Chili

ingredients

- 3 Tbsp. vegetable oil
- 2 pounds beef or pork, cubed
- 12-ounce bottle beer
- 2 scotch bonnet chiles, unseeded, minced
- 1 large onion, chopped
- 1 stalk celery, minced
- ½ green bell pepper, chopped
- 2 cloves garlic, minced
- 1 tsp. ground coriander
- 1 tsp. paprika
- 1 tsp. ground cumin
- 1 tsp. sugar
- 1 Tbsp. fresh lime juice
- 1 Tbsp. masa harina or cornmeal
- about 1 tsp. salt

Made with scotch bonnet chiles, one of the hottest chiles on earth, this chili is searingly hot. Serve it with rice to absorb the sauce. Equally hot habanero chiles can be substituted.

● Heat 1 tablespoon of the oil in a skillet and brown the meat. Put the meat and beer in a large saucepan to simmer. Heat the remaining 2 tablespoons oil in the skillet and sauté the chiles, onion, celery, bell pepper, and garlic 5 minutes. Add to the meat with the remaining ingredients, except the masa harina and salt.

● Bring to a boil, reduce heat, cover and simmer at least 1 hour, adding water or beer if necessary. Mix the masa harina or cornmeal with a little warm water to make a smooth paste and add it to the chili to thicken. Add salt to taste.

Hair-on-your-chest Chili

ingredients

- 8 ounces pork sausage
- 2 pounds pork, cubed
- 12-ounce bottle beer
- 2 cups beef stock
- 1 Tbsp. vegetable oil
- 1½ medium onions, chopped
- 3 Anaheim chiles
- 2 canned chipotle chiles
- 2 habanero chiles, unseeded, minced
- 2 Tbsp. chili powder
- 2 tsp. ground cumin
- 1 tsp. dried oregano
- 1 tsp. ground coriander seed
- 1 tsp. black pepper
- 1 Tbsp. masa harina
- about 1 tsp. salt
- 1 shot (3 Tbsp.) tequila

Here is a chili that will test the asbestos palate and stomach of chili-lovers who boast about how hot they like their chili. It is made with habanero chiles, the hottest chiles on earth. The only substitute is the equally incendiary scotch bonnet chile. This chili also uses chipotle chiles – smoked jalapeños – but just for the smoky flavor, since the jalapeño is mild in comparison to the habanero. It's finished off with a shot of tequila.

● Crumble the sausage into a skillet and fry until a little fat has rendered out. Add the cubed pork and cook until the meat has browned. Put the meat in a large pot with the beer and beef stock. Bring to a boil, reduce heat and simmer. Discard any fat from skillet. Heat the oil in the skillet and sauté the onion 5 minutes. Add the onion to the pork.

● Roast the Anaheim chiles under a broiler until the skin has blackened and blistered on all sides. Put the chiles in a paper bag, covered heat-proof bowl, or foil pouch, and seal. After the chiles have steamed in the bag, bowl, or foil for 10 minutes, remove them. Peel the chiles and remove the stems and seeds. Put the Anaheim chiles in a blender or food processor. Remove the stems from the chipotles, and add them to the Anaheims. To add volume, add a little bit of the chili cooking liquid. Purée until smooth. If you don't want to chop the habaneros by hand, add them to the blender after the mixture is puréed. Blend or process in just a few short bursts – the habaneros should be chopped but not puréed. Add the chile mixture to the stew.

● Add the chili powder, cumin, oregano, coriander, and black pepper. Let the chili continue simmering – the meat should cook for a minimum of 1½ hours. When the chili is well cooked, mix the masa harina with 2 tablespoons cold water to make a paste, then add the paste to the chili. Add salt, taste, and adjust seasonings. Add the tequila and serve.

▶ *Hair-on-your-chest Chili*

Teary-eyed Beef and Pork Chili

MAKES 4 SERVINGS

This hot chili gets its heat from pure ground chile de arbol powder. This is a purist's chili – nothing but meat, onion, and sauce that is full of flavor.

ingredients

- 3 Tbsp. vegetable oil
- 1 pound beef, cubed
- 1 pound pork, cubed
- 1½ cups beef stock
- 1½ onions, chopped
- 8-ounce can tomato sauce
- 1 tsp. celery salt
- 1 tsp. garlic powder
- 2 Tbsp. commercial chili powder
- 1 tsp. pure chile de arbol powder
- 2 tsp. ground cumin
- 1 tsp. dried marjoram
- ½ tsp. sugar
- 1 Tbsp. masa harina
- 1–2 tsp. salt

● Heat 1 tablespoon of the oil in a large skillet and cook the beef and pork until browned. Remove the meat with a slotted spoon and put it in a large pot with the beef stock. Bring to a boil, reduce heat and simmer. Discard greasy cooking liquids from the skillet.

● Heat remaining 2 tablespoons oil in the skillet and sauté the onion 5 minutes. Add the onion to the meat with the remaining ingredients, except the masa harina and salt. Simmer the chili at least 1 hour. Mix the masa harina with 2 tablespoons water to form a paste. Add the paste to the chili and stir well. Add salt, taste, and adjust seasonings.

Three Flames Beef Chili

MAKES 4 SERVINGS

*T*his is a very hot chili, but toasting the cumin and oregano enhances their flavors so they are not drowned out by the heat of three pure chile powders – the hot chile de arbol and cayenne, and the milder pasilla.

- Cook the bacon in a skillet. When done, set it on paper towels to drain and cool. You will need about 3 tablespoons of drippings – discard any excess.
- Reheat 1 tablespoon of the bacon drippings and cook the beef until browned. Remove the beef. Add up to 2 tablespoons bacon drippings and heat. Add the onion, bell pepper, and garlic, and sauté 5 minutes. Put the beef and sautéed vegetables in a large saucepan. Add the beer, tomato sauce, and chile powders. Bring to a boil, reduce heat and simmer.

- Heat a small skillet and add the cumin seeds and oregano. Cook, gently shaking the pan occasionally so they do not scorch, until they are brown. Remove and grind in a mortar and pestle, a small grinder, or place them between two sheets of wax paper and crush with the edge of a rolling pin. Add to the chili with the sugar.
- Simmer the meat at least 1½ hours. Just before serving, crumble the bacon and add. Add the salt, taste, and adjust seasonings.

ingredients

- **4 strips of bacon**
- **2 pounds beef, cubed**
- **1½ medium onions, chopped**
- **½ green bell pepper, finely chopped**
- **4 cloves garlic, minced**
- **12-ounce bottle of beer**
- **8-ounce can tomato sauce**
- **1 Tbsp. pure chile de arbol powder**
- **2 Tbsp. pure pasilla chile powder**
- **½ tsp. cayenne**
- **2 tsp. whole cumin seeds**
- **2 tsp. dried oregano**
- **½ tsp. sugar**
- **about 1 tsp. salt**

Terry's Chili for the Tender Palate

MAKES 4 SERVINGS

ingredients

3 Tbsp. vegetable oil

2 pounds beef, cubed

1 medium onion, chopped

4 cloves garlic, minced

2 cups beef stock

8-ounce can tomato sauce

3 Tbsp. commercial chili powder

2 tsp. dried oregano

about 1 tsp. salt

My husband grew up in Baltimore. By the time he moved to Austin, Texas, Terry was an adult who had never developed a taste for spicy food. He left Texas less than three years later with a story about a woman and debts, but I believe the truth is that he was run out one night when he made the mistake of telling a Texan he didn't like chili. Here is a mild chili I make just for him. It is delicious over steamed white rice.

● Heat 1 tablespoon of the oil in a skillet and cook the beef until browned on all sides. With a slotted spoon, remove the beef to a large saucepan. Discard the fatty cooking liquids. Heat the remaining 2 tablespoons oil in the skillet and sauté the onion and garlic 5 minutes. Add the onion and garlic to the beef. Add the remaining ingredients, except salt.

● Bring to a boil, reduce heat and simmer at least 1½ hours, adding water or beef stock if needed. Add salt, taste, and adjust seasonings.

New Mexico Chili with Lamb

MAKES 4 TO 6 SERVINGS

ingredients

2 Tbsp. vegetable oil

2 pounds lamb, cubed

1½ medium onions, chopped

4 cloves garlic, minced

8 New Mexico, Anaheim, or poblano chiles or a combination

8-ounce can tomato sauce

2–4 jalapeño or serrano chiles, unseeded, minced

1 tsp. dried oregano

¼ tsp. dried sage

⅓ cup chopped fresh cilantro

about 1 tsp. salt

Lamb is a staple of the Navajo Indians of New Mexico and is frequently prepared in stews. Here it is paired with green chiles. Fresh New Mexico green chiles are traditional, but Anaheim or poblano chiles or a combination can be substituted. The jalapeño or serrano chiles add the heat. The strong flavor of lamb overwhelms a mild chili and is best in a very spicy-hot stew. Serve with Navajo fry bread or plain steamed rice.

● In a large, deep skillet, heat the oil and cook the lamb until browned on all sides. If the skillet is large enough, add the onion and garlic and cook 5 minutes longer, then transfer to a large pot. If the skillet is not large enough, remove the lamb to a large pot. Add additional oil to the skillet, if needed. Sauté the onion and garlic 5 minutes, then add to the lamb. Add about 3 cups water. Bring the stew to a boil, reduce heat and simmer at least 1½ hours. Add water if needed.

● While the lamb is simmering, roast the green chiles (but not the jalapeños or serranos). Place them under a broiler and cook, turning, until all sides are blistered and blackened. Remove the chiles and immediately put them in a paper bag or covered bowl to steam for at least 10 minutes. Peel the chiles and remove the stems and seeds.

● Chop half the chiles and add them to the stew. Put the other half in a blender or food processor with the tomato sauce and purée until smooth. Add the purée to the stew, along with the jalapeños or serranos, the oregano, and sage. About 10 minutes before the chili is done, add the fresh cilantro and salt. Taste and adjust seasonings.

▼ *New Mexico Chili with Lamb*

Beef and Sausage Chili

MAKES 4 TO 6 SERVINGS

The seasonings in the Italian sausage add an extra dimension of flavor to this basic moderate chili. To adjust the heat, increase or decrease the amount of Tabasco sauce.

ingredients

8 ounces Italian-style pork sausage

2 pounds beef, cubed

1 medium onion, chopped

1 green bell pepper, chopped

2 cloves garlic, minced

2 cups beef broth

8-ounce can tomato sauce

2 Tbsp. commercial chili powder

2 tsp. ground cumin

about 1 tsp. Tabasco or other hot pepper sauce

about 1 tsp. salt

● Crumble the sausage into a large, deep skillet and cook about 2 minutes, until some of the fat has rendered out. Add the beef and cook, turning occasionally, until the meat is lightly browned. Spoon off the excess fat. Add the onion, bell pepper, and garlic and cook 5 minutes.

● Transfer the mixture to a large saucepan. Add the remaining ingredients, except salt. Bring to a boil, reduce heat and simmer until the meat is tender, about 1½ hours. Add water as needed. Add salt, taste, and adjust seasonings.

Jalapeño Chili

MAKES 4 SERVINGS

This is a hot but simple chili, seasoned with chili powder and unseeded fresh jalapeños. To reduce the heat, remove the seeds and veins from the jalapeños.

ingredients

2 Tbsp. vegetable oil

2 pounds beef or pork, cubed

1 medium onion, chopped

6 jalapeño chiles, unseeded, minced

2 cloves garlic, minced

2 cups beef stock

8-ounce can tomato sauce

2 Tbsp. commercial chili powder

1 tsp. ground cumin

1 tsp. dried oregano

about 1 tsp salt

● Heat 1 tablespoon of the oil in a skillet and cook the meat until browned. Remove the meat with a slotted spoon. Discard the greasy cooking liquids. Heat the remaining a tablespoon of oil and sauté the onion, jalapeños, and garlic 5 minutes.

● Put the meat, vegetables, beef stock, and 1 cup water in a large saucepan. Stir in the tomato sauce, chili powder, cumin, and oregano. Bring to a boil, reduce heat and simmer at least 1½ hours until the meat is tender. Stir occasionally and add water if needed. Add salt, taste, and adjust seasonings.

Scorcher Chili

This chili is for Texas purists – those who want no beans and no tomatoes in a scorchingly hot but simple chili. The beer-based sauce gets its heat from pure chile de arbol powder and unseeded jalapeños, while pasilla and mild New Mexico or California pure chile powders fill out the chile flavor.

● Heat 1 tablespoon of the oil in a skillet and cook the beef until browned. With a slotted spoon, remove the meat. Discard the greasy cooking liquids. Heat the remaining 1 tablespoon oil in the skillet and sauté the onion 5 minutes. Put the beef, onion, and beer in a large pot. While the mixture is heating, dissolve the bouillon cubes in 1 cup hot water. Add the bouillon water plus 2 cups water to the meat. Bring to a boil. Add the remaining ingredients, except the masa harina and salt. Simmer until the meat is tender, at least 1½ hours, adding water if needed.

● Mix the masa harina with 3 tablespoons water and stir to make a paste. Add to the chili and cook 2 minutes. Add salt, taste, and adjust seasonings.

ingredients

2 Tbsp. vegetable oil

2 pounds beef, cubed

1 onion, chopped

12-ounce bottle beer

2 beef bouillon cubes

3 jalapeño chiles, unseeded, minced

1 Tbsp. pure pasilla chile powder

1 Tbsp. mild New Mexico or California chile powder

1 tsp. chile de arbol powder

2 tsp. ground cumin

2 tsp. ground oregano

1 tsp. garlic powder

1 tsp. ground coriander

2 Tbsp. masa harina

about ½ tsp. salt

◄ *Scorcher Chili*

Simple Beef and Salsa Chili

MAKES 4 SERVINGS

ingredients

2 Tbsp. vegetable oil

2 pounds beef, cubed

1 medium onion, chopped

2 cups bottled red salsa, preferably chunky

8-ounce can tomato sauce

2 beef bouillon cubes

3 Tbsp. commercial chili powder

1 tsp. ground cumin

1 tsp. dried oregano

cayenne to taste

salt, if needed

This is a very easy-to-make chili, with bottled salsa providing the heart of the sauce. The spiciness will depend on the type of salsa you use, but can be increased by adding cayenne. The salsa and bouillon may provide enough salt.

● Heat 1 tablespoon of the oil in a skillet and cook the beef until lightly browned. Remove the meat with a slotted spoon. Discard the greasy cooking liquids. Heat the remaining 1 tablespoon oil in the skillet and sauté the onion 5 minutes.

● Put the beef, onion, salsa, and tomato sauce in a large saucepan. Dissolve the bouillon cubes in 2 cups hot water and add to the chili. Add the chili powder, cumin, and oregano. Bring to a boil, reduce heat and simmer until the meat is tender, about 1½ hours. Stir occasionally, adding water if needed. If desired, add cayenne and salt to taste.

Chili Verde Stew

MAKES 4 TO 6 SERVINGS

Although I grew up in Southern California where spices are added with a heavy hand, for many years my experience with fresh chiles was fairly limited. One day I was experimenting with a recipe for green chile stew. It called for poblano chiles, described as green and triangular. My local grocery store had a large selection of fresh chiles, but a single sign that said only "red and green chiles." The produce clerk pointed out the poblanos. To me, they looked like jalapeños, but they were green and somewhat triangular, so I bought a dozen. I roasted and peeled them, and added them to the stew, seeds and all. Then I sampled it. I thought the skin was going to wither right off my tongue! It was the hottest food I'd ever put in my mouth. At dinner, none of us could stand the scorchingly hot stew, so we just ate cornbread, chile con queso, and tortilla chips. Of course the chiles were jalapeños – a few days later, a friend introduced me to poblanos, which look nothing like jalapeños. Made with poblanos, the stew is pleasantly spicy.

● Roast the chiles under the broiler, turning often with tongs, until they are almost totally black, about 10 minutes. Put the chiles in a plastic or paper bag, close the bag, and let them sit for 20 minutes. Remove them one by one, stem and seed them and cut them into strips.

● Dredge the meat in the flour. Heat 1 tablespoon of the shortening in a large skillet and brown the meat. Put the meat in a large pot. Heat the remaining shortening and sauté the onions and garlic. Add them, with the rest of the ingredients, to the stew pot. Add 2 cups of water. Simmer the stew over low heat for 1 hour.

ingredients

10–12 poblano chiles

2 pounds pork butt or roast, cubed

¼ cup all-purpose flour

2 Tbsp. shortening

2 large onions, chopped

4 cloves garlic, minced

2 cups whole canned tomatoes, coarsely chopped

8-ounce can tomato sauce

1 tsp. salt

dash of black pepper

Eye-popping Chili with Corn

MAKES 4 TO 6 SERVINGS

This chili starts with a hot bottled salsa and gets hotter with New Mexico chile powder. The corn adds a pleasing sweetness and a bit of crunch. If you have fresh corn, hold it over the pot as you cut the corn off the cob so that the milky liquid drips into the chili. Otherwise, frozen corn is fine.

ingredients

- 3 Tbsp. vegetable oil
- 1½ cups bottled hot salsa
- 2 beef bouillon cubes
- 1 medium onion, chopped
- 2 pounds beef, cubed or coarsely ground
- 2 Tbsp. hot New Mexico chile powder
- 2 Tbsp. commercial chili powder
- 1 tsp. ground cumin
- 1 tsp. dried oregano
- 1 tsp. garlic powder
- 1 tsp. celery salt
- 1 cup corn (about two ears)
- about 1 tsp. salt

● Heat 1 tablespoon of the oil in a large saucepan. When the oil is sizzling hot, add the salsa and fry 5 minutes. Dissolve the bouillon cubes in 1 cup boiling water and add it to the salsa, with 2 more cups water.

● Heat 1 tablespoon of the oil in a skillet and sauté the onion 5 minutes. Add the onion to the salsa. Heat the remaining oil and cook the beef until lightly browned. Add to the salsa with the remaining ingredients, except the corn and salt. Simmer 1 hour. Add the corn and simmer 30 minutes. Add salt, taste, and adjust seasonings.

Savory Beef Chili

Small amounts of unsweetened cocoa and cinnamon are the secret ingredients in this tasty chili. Your kitchen may smell like cappuccino, but the ingredients will remain a mystery in the chili. Cocoa deepens the flavor of the sauce, giving it rich undertones.

● Heat 1 tablespoon of the oil in a skillet and cook the beef until browned. Remove the meat with a slotted spoon and discard the greasy cooking liquids. Heat the remaining 2 tablespoons oil in the skillet and sauté the onion, celery, bell pepper, and garlic 5 minutes.

● Put the beef and vegetables in a large saucepan with the beer, tomato sauce, and 2 cups water. Add jalapeños, bay leaves, chili powder, cocoa, and cinnamon. Bring to a boil, reduce heat and simmer until the pork is tender, at least 1½ hours. Stir occasionally and add water if needed.

● Add the lime juice and Tabasco sauce and cook 5 minutes. Add salt, taste, and adjust seasonings.

ingredients

3 Tbsp. vegetable oil

2 pounds beef, cubed

1½ onions, chopped

1 stalk celery, finely chopped

½ green bell pepper, finely chopped

2 cloves garlic, minced

12-ounce bottle beer

8-ounce can tomato sauce

2 jalapeño chiles, unseeded, minced

2 bay leaves

3 Tbsp. commercial chili powder

2 tsp. unsweetened cocoa

⅛ tsp. ground cinnamon

1 Tbsp. lime juice

at least ½ tsp. Tabasco or other hot pepper sauce

1–2 tsp. salt

Pork and Chorizo Chili

This is a very hearty chili with bold flavors. Made with a combination of two dried California chiles, two dried New Mexico chiles, and two dried chiles negros, it is hot but not fiery. Vary the chiles to suit your taste.

ingredients

6 large dried chiles, such as New Mexico, California, anchos, or a combination

3 Tbsp. vegetable oil

2 pounds pork, cubed

1½ medium onions, chopped

1 stalk celery, finely chopped

⅓ green bell pepper, chopped

4 cloves garlic, minced

2 beef bouillon cubes

2 tsp. ground cumin

2 tsp. dried oregano

1 tsp. ground coriander

⅛ tsp. dried sage

½ tsp. sugar

8 ounces chorizo sausage (unsmoked)

2 Tbsp. masa harina

1–2 tsp. salt

● Remove the stems and seeds from the dried chiles. Cut each chile in several pieces, place in a small heat-proof bowl and add 1 cup boiling water. Stir to be sure all pieces of chiles are covered. Let soak 30 minutes.

● Meanwhile, heat 1 tablespoon of the oil in a skillet and cook the pork, stirring occasionally, until lightly browned. Remove the meat with a slotted spoon and discard the greasy cooking liquids. Heat the remaining 2 tablespoons oil in the skillet and sauté the onion, celery, bell pepper, and garlic 5 minutes.

● Put the pork and vegetables in a large saucepan and add water to cover. Bring to a boil, reduce heat and simmer. Dissolve the bouillon cubes in 1 cup hot water and add to the chili. Add the cumin, oregano, coriander, sage, and sugar.

● Put the dried chiles and their soaking liquid in a blender or food processor. Purée until smooth. Strain to remove seeds and bits of skin and discard solids. Add the sauce to the chili.

● After the chili has cooked about 1 hour, crumble the chorizo into a hot skillet and fry 7 to 8 minutes, until all the fat has rendered out. Remove from the heat and tilt the pan to drain the fat. With a slotted spoon, remove the chorizo and add to the chili. Discard the fat.

● Continue simmering until the pork is tender, at least 1½ hours, adding water if needed. When the chili is ready, dissolve the masa harina in ¼ cup cold water to make a paste. Add to the chili and stir well. Add salt, taste, and adjust seasonings.

California Chili Buffet

This buffet starts with a spicy Texas-style chili with ground beef, cubed beef, cubed pork, and pork sausage, but it becomes a California-style meal with such trimmings as black olives, Avocado Salsa, and goat cheese. Serve the chili next to a big pot of black beans, and let guests add their own toppings.

ingredients

BUFFET:

Chili, Smoky Black Beans (page 110) or Hot Black Beans (page 110), grated Monterey jack cheese, crumbled goat cheese, sliced black olives, Avocado Salsa (page 122), chopped onions, chopped fresh cilantro , chopped jalapeño chiles, and sour cream.

CHILI:

4–6 Tbsp. vegetable oil

2 pounds beef, cubed

2 pounds pork, cubed

2 pounds ground beef

1 pound pork sausage

2 large onions, chopped

8 cloves garlic, minced

6 cups beef stock

16-ounce can tomato paste

4 tsp. whole cumin seed

1 Tbsp. dried oregano

1 tsp. dried basil

1 tsp. celery seed

1 tsp. coriander seed

½ cup commercial chili powder

3 Tbsp. hot New Mexico chile powder

juice of 1 lime

1 tsp. sugar

1–3 tsp. salt

● You will need to cook the meat in batches. Unless you have a really large skillet, don't cook more than 1½ pounds at a time. You can mix the cubed beef and pork or the ground beef and sausage, but don't try to cook ground meat with cubed meat. The ground meat does not need to be cooked in oil. Heat about 1 tablespoon oil for each batch of cubed meat. Put the cooked meat in a large stockpot, but don't put it on the heat until you add liquid.

● After cooking the meats, heat 2 tablespoons oil in the skillet and sauté the onion and garlic for 5 minutes. Add the onion to the pot with the meat. Add the beef stock and tomato paste and stir well. Bring to a boil,then reduce heat and simmer about 1½ hours.

● In a small, dry skillet, add the cumin seed, oregano, basil, celery seed, and coriander seed. Toast over medium heat, shaking the pan frequently so the seeds don't scorch. Cook until the seeds are fragrant and lightly toasted, but take care that they do not burn. Remove from the heat and let seeds cool 5 to 10 minutes. Grind them in a nut grinder, mortar and pestle, or crush them with the edge of a rolling pin. Add to the chili. Add the chili powders, mix well, and let the stew continue simmering.

● About 30 minutes before the chili is done, add the lime juice and sugar, and continue simmering. When the meat is very tender, add salt, taste, and adjust seasonings.

Donna Roberts' Hearty Venison Chili

MAKES 4 TO 6 SERVINGS

ingredients

2 pounds ground venison

2 medium onions, chopped

4 cloves garlic, minced

16-ounce can tomato sauce

4 Tbsp. chili powder

1 tsp. ground cumin

½ tsp. cayenne

2 tsp. Worcestershire sauce

1½ tsp. salt

5 whole cloves

2 tsp. allspice

My husband, who loves to write about cars as much as I love to write about food, was interviewing Ross Roberts, vice president and general manager of Ford Motor Company, when he mentioned that I was working on a chili cookbook. Roberts, a Texan who loves chili, sent me this recipe for his wife's chili. The cloves and allspice complement the venison, while the chili powder and cayenne make a pleasantly spicy chili.

● Cover the meat with water and cook in a large saucepan, stirring until the meat crumbles. Stir in all the remaining ingredients. Cook for 30 minutes at medium heat. Simmer, covered, for 2 hours. Keep checking until the chili is the desired consistency.

Turkey Chili

MAKES 6 SERVINGS

ingredients

2 dried chiles negros

2 dried Anaheim (California) chiles

2–3 Tbsp. vegetable oil

6 ounces turkey sausage

1 pound ground turkey

1 medium onion, chopped

1 stalk celery, chopped

2 cups chicken broth

8 ounces tomato sauce

1 tsp. ground cumin

1 tsp. dried oregano

¼ tsp. cayenne or to taste

15-ounce can frijoles colorados, drained (small red beans)

about 1 tsp. salt

This is a very hearty chili with bold flavors. It is moderately hot, made with dried Anaheim chiles, chiles negroes and a little cayenne, but other large dried chiles can be substituted. Ground turkey and turkey sausage provide a lower-fat alternative to beef and pork, but check the packaging to be sure ground turkey and turkey sausage contain 10 percent fat or less. Some turkey products contain a lot of turkey fat and skin, giving them a higher fat content than ground pork or beef.

● Remove the stems and seeds from the chiles, then cut each chile in several pieces. Put the pieces in a small heat-proof bowl and add 1 cup boiling water. Stir to be sure all the pieces of chile are covered by water. Let soak 30 minutes.

● Meanwhile, put about 1 teaspoon oil in a large skillet and crumble in the turkey sausage. If, after 2 or 3 minutes, the sausage doesn't render any additional fat, add about 2 teaspoons more oil to the skillet. Crumble the ground turkey into the skillet. Cook until the meat is lightly browned. Remove from the pan.

● Heat 1½ tablespoons oil in the skillet and sauté onion and celery 5 minutes.

Put the meat and vegetables in a large saucepan and add the chicken broth, tomato sauce, and spices. Bring to a boil, reduce heat and simmer.

● Put the chiles and soaking liquid in a blender or food processor and purée until smooth. Strain to remove seeds and bits of skin, and discard solids. Add the sauce to the chili.

● Simmer the chili at least 1 hour, adding water or chicken broth if needed. Add the beans and cook 5 minutes. Add salt, taste, and adjust seasonings.

▲ *Turkey Chili*

Beef and Chorizo Chili

MAKES 5 TO 6 SERVINGS

ingredients

- 3 Tbsp. vegetable oil
- 2 pounds beef, cubed
- 1½ medium onions, chopped
- 1 stalk celery, finely chopped
- 3 cloves garlic, minced
- 2 beef bouillon cubes
- 8-ounce can tomato sauce
- 2 Tbsp. commercial chili powder
- 2 Tbsp. "hot" or "Mexican" chili powder
- 1 tsp. dried oregano
- 12 ounces chorizo sausage (unsmoked)
- about 1 tsp. salt
- ¼ cup fresh cilantro, chopped
- ⅓ cup green onions, chopped

Chorizo, a Spanish pork sausage, gives this chili a richer flavor. It is a moderately hot, robust chili that uses regular chili powder and "hot" or "Mexican" chili powder, but no cumin other than that in the two chili powder blends. Fresh cilantro and green onion added at the end provide a nice contrast in flavor and texture.

● Heat 1 tablespoon of the oil in a skillet and cook the beef until brown. Remove the meat with a slotted spoon and set aside. Discard the greasy cooking liquid. Heat the remaining 2 tablespoons oil in the skillet and sauté the onion, celery, and garlic 5 minutes. Put the cooked beef and vegetables in a large saucepan and barely cover with water. Bring to a boil, reduce heat and simmer. Dissolve the bouillon cubes in 1 cup hot water, and add to the chili. Add the tomato sauce, chili powders, and oregano to the chili. Occasionally stir the chili, adding water if needed.

● After the chili has cooked about 1 hour, crumble the chorizo into a skillet and cook over medium heat 7 to 8 minutes, until all the fat is rendered out. Remove the skillet from the heat and tilt to drain the fat. Remove the sausage with a slotted spoon and add to the chili. Discard the fat.

● Continue simmering the chili until the beef is tender, a total of at least 1½ hours. Just before serving, add salt, taste, and adjust seasonings. Stir in the cilantro and green onions.

Walt and Carolyn's Texas Bowl of Red

MAKES 6 SERVINGS

ingredients

3 pounds brisket

2–3 ounces kidney suet

3 heaping Tbsp. Gebhart's chili powder

1 Tbsp. dried oregano

1 Tbsp. ground cumin

1 Tbsp. cayenne

1 Tbsp. salt

1 Tbsp. Tabasco sauce

6–8 cloves garlic, minced

I grew up thinking of chili as a mild mixture of ground beef and kidney beans. Walt Wiley, a transplanted Texan and my co-worker on a California newspaper, was the first to tell me the Texas side of the chili story. True chili has no beans, no tomatoes, no onions, and is never mild. His wife, Carolyn, a gourmet cook, adapted this recipe from one in Frank X. Tolbert's classic "A Bowl of Red". They suggest serving it with saltines, or putting it over a mound of Fritos to make Frito Pie, a teenage favorite. "We found that chili made like this was a lot like the chili we remembered from our childhoods in North Texas," Walt said. "You could get a bowl for a quarter at the bus station or any greasy spoon cafe."

● Trim the fat off the brisket and cut the brisket into cubes about the size of the end of your thumb. Chop up and render the kidney suet and brown the brisket in that. Put the meat and fat in a pot with enough water to cover the meat 1 inch or so. Add the chili powder. Bring to a boil, reduce heat and let simmer ½ hour. Add oregano, cumin, cayenne, salt, Tabasco, and garlic.

● Let the chili simmer another 45 minutes or so. Don't stir it too much and don't let it boil dry and scorch, but don't add so much water that it is soupy. There will be a lot of grease, which probably should be skimmed.

Texas Waterfront Chipotle Pork Chili

MAKES 4 SERVINGS

This chili is made with Anaheim and chipotle chiles, but it will be the chipotles that will make you want to throw yourself in the river to cool off. This is a true Texas chili, made with no beans and no tomatoes, thickened with cracker crumbs.

● Heat 2 tablespoons of the oil in a large skillet and sauté the onion and garlic 5 minutes. Remove the onion to a large saucepan and set aside. Heat the remaining oil and cook the pork until lightly browned on all sides. Add the pork to the saucepan, then the chicken broth. Bring to a boil, stirring well, then reduce heat and simmer, adding water if needed.

● Roast the Anaheim chiles under a broiler, turning until the skin on all sides is blistered and mostly blackened. Remove from the broiler and put in a paper bag, a foil envelope, or a small covered bowl.

Let steam at least 10 minutes. Peel off the skin and remove the seeds. Cut each chile across its width into several pieces. Put the Anaheims in a blender or food processor. Remove the stems from the chipotles, add them to the Anaheims and purée. Add the purée to the chili. Add the remaining ingredients, except the cracker crumbs and salt.

● When the meat has simmered 1½ hours, add the cracker crumbs to thicken. Taste, add salt if needed, and adjust seasonings.

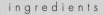

ingredients

- **3 Tbsp. vegetable oil**
- **1½ medium onions, chopped**
- **3 cloves garlic, minced**
- **2 pounds pork, diced**
- **2 cups chicken broth**
- **4 Anaheim chiles**
- **4 canned chipotle chiles**
- **1 Tbsp. commercial chili powder**
- **1 tsp. ground cumin**
- **2 tsp. dried oregano**
- **about 2 Tbsp. cracker crumbs (crushed saltines will do)**
- **about ½ tsp. salt**

Pork Chili with Corn and Jalapeños

MAKES 6 TO 8 SERVINGS

ingredients

3 Tbsp. vegetable oil
2 pounds pork, diced
1 pound pork sausage
1½ medium onions, chopped
1 stalk celery, finely chopped
½ green bell pepper, finely chopped
3 cloves garlic, minced
2 beef bouillon cubes
3 Tbsp. commercial chili powder
1 Tbsp. ancho chile powder
1 tsp. ground cumin
1 tsp. dried oregano
1 cup corn (about 2 ears)
2 jalapeño chiles, minced
2 Tbsp. fresh cilantro, chopped
about 1 tsp. salt

This is a moderately hot chili if you don't remove the seeds and veins from the jalapeños, a pleasantly spicy chili if you remove them. It is thick with vegetables, including corn, which adds a slight sweetness. Use frozen corn or fresh, cut straight from the cob into the pot.

● Heat 1 tablespoon of the oil in a large skillet and cook the pork until lightly browned. Put the pork in a pot, but do not put it on the heat yet. Crumble the sausage into the skillet and cook until browned. Drain off and discard any grease. Add the sausage to the pork. Heat the remaining oil in the skillet and sauté the onions, celery, bell pepper, and garlic 5 minutes and add to the pork.

● Dissolve the bouillon cubes in 1 cup boiling water. Add to the pork with 2 more cups water. Add the spices to the pork, stir well. Bring to a boil, reduce heat and simmer until the pork is very tender, about 1½ hours.

● About 30 minutes before the chili is done, add the corn and jalapeños. About 5 minutes before it is done, add the cilantro. Add salt, taste, and adjust seasonings.

Bloody Mary Chili

MAKES 4 SERVINGS

ingredients

2 Tbsp. vegetable oil
1 medium onion, chopped
2 pounds beef, diced
2 cups beef stock
12 ounces tomato juice or Bloody Mary mix
1 Tbsp. mild New Mexico chile powder
1 Tbsp. hot chile powder
1 Tbsp. ancho chile powder
2 tsp. ground cumin
2 tsp. dried oregano
1 tsp. garlic powder
about 2 Tbsp. cracker crumbs

This is a moderately spicy chili seasoned with three pure chile powders and thickened with cracker crumbs.

● Heat 1 tablespoon of the oil in a skillet and sauté the onion 5 minutes. Remove the onion. Add the remaining oil and heat. Cook the beef until it is lightly browned.

● Put the onion, beef, and remaining ingredients, except the crumbs and salt, in a large saucepan. Stir well. Bring to a boil, reduce heat and simmer 1½ hours. Stir occasionally and add water if needed. Add the cracker crumbs to thicken. Add ½–1 teaspoon of salt, taste, and adjust seasonings.

▶ *Bloody Mary Chili*

Ground Beef and Turkey Chili with Three Chile Powders

MAKES 4 SERVINGS

The combination of California, ancho, and New Mexico chile powders provides a rich range of chile flavors. This is pleasantly spicy, and can be made hotter by adding New Mexico chile powder.

● Heat the oil in a skillet and sauté the onion and garlic 5 minutes. Put the vegetables in a large pot and set aside. Brown the beef, then the turkey in the skillet, adding each to the pot. Add the beef stock, 2 cups water, tomato sauce, and seasonings to the pot. Bring to a boil, stirring well. Reduce the heat and simmer 1 to 1½ hours, stirring occasionally and adding water if needed. Taste, adjust seasonings, and add salt if desired.

ingredients

1 Tbsp. vegetable oil

1 onion, chopped

4 cloves garlic, minced

1 pound ground beef

1 pound ground turkey

2 cups beef or chicken stock

8-ounce can tomato sauce

1 Tbsp. California chile powder

1 Tbsp. ancho chile powder

1 Tbsp. hot New Mexico chile powder

1 tsp. ground cumin

1 tsp. dried oregano

1 tsp. dried basil

1 tsp. celery salt

Cuisinart Chili

MAKES 4 SERVINGS

Many chili purists don't like the food processor. One minute you have an uneven mixture of chunks and chopped meat and vegetables, a few seconds later you have mush. But the food processor provides a solution for chili-lovers who don't have a meat grinder, don't live near a grocery store that sells chili-grind meat, and don't have the time to painstakingly cut the meat into tiny cubes. The secret is to use the pulse button and to chop in very short bursts. Add the onions, garlic, and jalapeños first, and process very briefly, then add the meat. If the seeds and veins are not removed from the jalapeños, this will be hot chili. For a milder chili, remove some or all of the seeds and veins. For extra flavor, substitute canned chipotle chiles for the jalapeños.

ingredients

1 large onion, chopped

3 cloves garlic, minced

3 jalapeño chiles

2 pounds chuck roast or other inexpensive cut of beef

3 Tbsp. vegetable oil

2 cups beef stock

8-ounce can tomato sauce

3 Tbsp. commercial chili powder

1 tsp. ground cumin

1 tsp. dried oregano

½ tsp. dried thyme

about 1 tsp. salt

● Cut the onion into eighths. Peel the garlic and cut each clove in half. Remove the stems from the jalapeños and cut into quarters. Remove any excess fat from the beef and cut beef into 8 or 10 chunks. Put the vegetables in food processor and pulse in two short bursts so vegetables are only partly chopped. Add the beef. Process in short bursts until the beef is coarsely chopped. A few large pieces of vegetable may need to be cut up by hand.

● Heat 1 tablespoon of the oil in a large skillet and cook half the beef-vegetable mixture until the meat is browned. Put the cooked mixture in a large saucepan and set aside. Heat the remaining oil and cook the remaining beef-vegetable mixture. Add it to the saucepan. Add the beef stock and tomato sauce. Bring to a boil, reduce heat. Add the spices and herbs, but not salt, and stir well. Simmer the chili 1½ hours, adding water or beef stock if needed. Taste, add salt, and adjust seasonings.

▲ *Cuisinart Chili*

Double Chile Chicken and Beef Chili

MAKES 10 TO 12 SERVINGS

With dried chile pods and chili powder, this chili has lots of chile flavor. Shredded chicken, ground beef, and cubed beef give it its hearty character. The heat will depend on the type of chile pods you use. California chiles will produce a mild chili, while New Mexico chiles will produce a fiery stew. I like to use a mix of California, ancho, and New Mexico chiles for a hot but not incendiary chili.

ingredients

- 2 chicken half-breasts, skin and excess fat removed
- 2 chicken bouillon cubes
- about ¼ cup vegetable oil
- 2 pounds beef, cubed
- 2 pounds ground beef
- 3 medium onions, chopped
- 8 cloves garlic, minced
- 10 dried chile pods
- 8-ounce can tomato sauce
- 5 tsp. ground cumin
- 4 tsp. dried oregano
- ¼ cup commercial chili powder
- 2 tsp. unsweetened cocoa
- 2–3 tsp. salt

● Put the chicken breasts in a medium saucepan. Cover with water, bring to a boil and cook 40 minutes. Remove the chicken from the broth and refrigerate the chicken. Pour the chicken broth into a large pot, add the bouillon cubes and simmer over low heat.

● Heat 1–2 tablespoons of the oil in a large skillet and cook the cubed beef (cook in batches if necessary) until lightly browned. Add to the chicken broth. Next, brown the ground beef, drain off fat, and add the beef to the chicken broth. Heat the remaining oil in the skillet and sauté the onions and garlic 5 minutes. Add to the chili.

● Remove the stems and seeds from the chile pods and cut the pods into several pieces. Put in a narrow, deep heat-proof bowl and pour 2 cups boiling water over the chiles. Stir to be sure all the chile pieces are covered by water. Let sit 30 minutes.

● Remove the chicken from the refrigerator. Shred the chicken and add to the chili with the tomato sauce.

● Pour the chiles and their soaking liquid into blender or food processor. Purée until smooth. Strain the sauce to remove seeds and bits of skin. Discard solids. Add the sauce to the chili. Add the remaining ingredients, except salt. Simmer, adding water if needed, until the cubed beef is very tender, about 1½ hours. Taste, adjust seasonings, and add salt.

Old West Jerky Chili

MAKES 4 SERVINGS

This chili is similar to the chili eaten in the Old West. It is made with beef jerky, dried and seasoned beef that kept well on the trail, and pure chile powders. Because the meat is dried, it will absorb more water than other chilis, so should be checked frequently and water added when needed. Most jerky is heavily salted, so little or no additional salt will be needed. That's also why pure chile powders are used, rather than commercial chili powder mixes, which contain salt.

● Chop the jerky into small pieces, keeping in mind that the pieces will swell as they absorb water. Heat the bacon drippings and cook the garlic and cumin seed 1 minute. Add the jerky and cook 3 minutes. Add 2 cups water, the chile powders, onion flakes, and oregano.

● Bring to a boil, reduce heat and simmer. Check often and add water as needed. Simmer at least 2 hours, then taste and adjust seasonings. To thicken the chili, mix the flour, masa, or cornmeal with 2 tablespoons cold water to make a paste, then add the paste to the chili. Cook, stirring, until thickened.

▼ *Old West Jerky Chili*

ingredients

- **6 ounces beef jerky**
- **3 Tbsp. bacon drippings**
- **2 cloves garlic, minced**
- **1 tsp. whole cumin seed**
- **2 Tbsp. California or mild New Mexico chile powder**
- **2 Tbsp. hot New Mexico chile powder**
- **1 Tbsp. dried onion flakes**
- **1 tsp. dried oregano**
- **2 Tbsp. flour, masa harina, or cornmeal**

3

CHILI WITH BEANS

Despite the insistence of chili purists that chili never includes beans, most of us were introduced to chili by way of a canned concoction of ground beef and beans. Many people who consider themselves chili-lovers have never had a true, no-beans bowl of Texas Red. Beans stretch the meat in chili; they also offer a balance to the spice and texture of the meaty stew. For people who believe beans are integral to chili, we offer the following 22 recipes.

Hayes' Venison and Black Bean Chili

MAKES 4 TO 6 SERVINGS

Hayes Johnson is a quintessential chili maker, and a teller of tall tales. The first time I met him, he introduced himself as a chilehead and bragged about the scotch bonnet chiles growing in pots on his patio. Hayes offered this recipe for "killer chili" as proof that his chili-making prowess is more than another tall tale. Hayes recommends serving this chili with Mexican cornbread and cold beer. Beef can substitute for the venison.

ingredients

- 2–3 Tbsp. olive oil
- 2–4 garlic cloves, minced
- 1 pound venison tenderloin, cut in thin strips
- 1 Tbsp. powdered beef bouillon
- garlic salt, black pepper, ground cayenne, ground cumin, crushed red pepper, to taste
- 1 large white onion, chopped
- 1 large green bell pepper, chopped
- 2–4 fresh hot chiles, preferably serrano or Thai, chopped
- 16-ounce can black beans, undrained
- 2 × 15-ounce cans whole tomatoes, undrained

● Heat the olive oil in a deep iron skillet and sauté the garlic over medium-high heat until it begins to brown. Add the venison and mix well to distribute the garlic. Stir frequently, cooking until all sides are brown. Add the beef bouillon. Add the spices to taste – don't be shy – and then stir in the chopped vegetables. Stir until coated with oil and beginning to soften.

● Stir the undrained beans and tomatoes into the mixture and bring to a rigorous boil. Stir frequently and boil on medium heat for 15 minutes or so. Reduce the heat to medium-low and cover the pot. Simmer 45 minutes to 1 hour, or until meat is tender and sauce is thick. If possible, cook several hours, or even a day, before needed. It gets better as it gets older.

Stretch-your-beef Chili Beans

MAKES 6 SERVINGS

*T*his economical chili uses only a small amount of beef, with kidney beans and lots of vegetables giving it substance. It is a thick, hot chili, but can be made milder by removing the veins and seeds from the jalapeños.

● Drain the kidney beans, put them in a large pot and cover with water. Bring to a boil, reduce heat and simmer.

● Heat 1 tablespoon of the oil in a skillet and brown the meat. Add the meat to the beans, discarding fat. Heat the remaining 2 tablespoons oil in the skillet and

sauté the onion, celery, bell pepper, and garlic 5 minutes. Add the vegetables to the beans. Add the remaining ingredients, except salt. Bring to a boil, reduce heat and simmer at least 1½ hours, adding water if needed. Add salt to taste.

ingredients

1 cup dry kidney beans, picked over and soaked overnight

3 Tbsp. vegetable oil

¾ pound beef, cut into ¼-inch dice

1½ onions, chopped

2 stalks celery, chopped

1 small green bell pepper, diced

4 cloves garlic, minced

15-ounce can tomatoes, chopped

8-ounce can tomato sauce

3 jalapeño chiles, unseeded, minced

1 tsp. ground cumin

1 tsp. dried oregano

1 tsp. paprika

½ tsp. ground coriander

2–3 beef bouillon cubes, crumbled

1–2 tsp. salt

Chunky Pork Chili with Beans

MAKES 6 SERVINGS

This hearty chili is mildly spicy but full of flavor.

ingredients

1 Tbsp. vegetable oil

2 pounds pork butt or shoulder, trimmed and cubed

1 onion, chopped

1 stalk celery, chopped

16 ounces tomato sauce

2 Tbsp. commercial chili powder

2 tsp. ground cumin

1 tsp. dried oregano

12-ounce bottle beer

4 ounces canned green chiles, chopped

1 tsp. sugar

1 tsp. salt

2 × 16-ounce cans kidney beans

● Heat the oil in a large pot and brown the meat lightly on all sides. Add the onion and celery and cook 5 minutes. Add the tomato sauce, spices, oregano, beer, and chiles.

● Bring the mixture to a boil. Cover, reduce heat and simmer 1 hour and 15 minutes, stirring occasionally and adding water if necessary. Add the sugar, salt, and beans, and cook 10 minutes. Taste and adjust seasonings.

White Chili with Chicken

MAKES 6 SERVINGS

This is a low-fat, moderately spicy chili, made with chicken, white beans, and Anaheim chiles.

ingredients

2 cups white beans, picked over and soaked overnight

1 Tbsp. chili powder

½ tsp. ground cumin

½ tsp. dried thyme

½ tsp. dried oregano

½ tsp. cayenne

½ tsp. garlic powder

1 Tbsp. flour

3 chicken half-breasts, cut into ½-inch cubes

2 Tbsp. vegetable oil

1 onion, chopped

1 stalk celery, chopped

2 cups chicken stock

4 Anaheim chiles, roasted, peeled and chopped, or 4-ounce can chopped green chiles

about 1 tsp. salt

¼ cup fresh cilantro, chopped

● Drain the beans, put them in a large pot and barely cover with fresh water. Bring to a boil, reduce heat and simmer.

● Mix the spices, herbs, seasonings, and flour. Toss the spice mix with the cubed chicken so the meat is evenly coated with spices, set aside. Heat 1 tablespoon of the oil in a skillet and sauté the onion and celery 6 minutes. Add the vegetables to the beans. Heat the remaining 1 tablespoon oil in a skillet and cook the chicken, turning often, until all sides are lightly browned. Add the chicken to the beans with the chicken stock and chiles. Simmer until the beans are tender, about 1½ hours total, adding water or chicken stock if needed. Add salt to taste and adjust seasonings. Add the cilantro just before serving.

▶ *White Chili with Chicken*

Chili Beans with Hamburger

ingredients

- 1 pound lean ground beef
- 1 medium onion, chopped
- 1 stalk celery, chopped
- ½ green bell pepper, chopped
- 1 clove garlic, minced
- 1 Tbsp. chili powder
- 1 tsp. dried oregano
- ½ tsp. cayenne
- 14½-ounce can tomatoes, chopped
- 8-ounce can tomato sauce
- 15-ounce can kidney beans

This simple chili is similar to canned chili con carne with ground beef and beans, only better. It is a hot chili, although not fiery.

● Brown the ground beef in a skillet. Remove the meat and set aside. Discard all but 1 tablespoon fat. Add the onion, celery, and bell pepper to the fat and sauté 5 minutes. Add the garlic, and sauté 1 minute. Put the vegetables and beef in a pot with the chili powder, oregano, cayenne, tomatoes, and tomato sauce. Mix well, bring to a boil, reduce heat and simmer 15 minutes. Add the beans and 1 teaspoon of salt. Cook 5 minutes. Taste and adjust seasonings.

Bob French's Colorado Chili

ingredients

- 2 cups dry Colorado frijoles, picked over
- ¼ pound salt pork
- 1 link (about 4 ounces) mild Italian sausage
- 1 pound ground beef
- ¾ medium onion, chopped
- 1 clove garlic, minced
- 2 Tbsp. commercial chili powder
- 1 Tbsp. flour
- 1 tsp. salt
- ½ tsp. ground cumin
- ½ tsp. sugar
- 8-ounce can tomato sauce
- 1 cup beer
- 3 shakes of Tabasco sauce
- 1 green bell pepper, diced
- 1 fresh Anaheim chile, diced

Bob French is a transplanted Coloradoan, now living in Florida, who is reminded of home when he makes this moderately spicy chili, which he recommends serving with cornbread. He and his wife, Virginia, also make this chili without the beans and pour it over the top of lightly scrambled eggs. Colorado frijoles are small red beans.

● Rinse and drain the beans. Add the beans and salt pork to 2 quarts water in a large pot. Bring to a boil and let boil for 2 minutes. Remove from heat and partially cover with a lid. Let stand 1 hour. Bring again to a boil and then reduce heat to simmer. Cover tightly and let simmer 1 hour. Drain, saving about 2 cups of the bean liquid.

● Cut off the end of the Italian sausage and squeeze out the sausage. Break up the sausage into a skillet and brown it with the ground beef. Drain off the fat. If the skillet is large enough, add the beans and remaining ingredients, except bean liquid. Otherwise, transfer the meat to the bean pot and add the beans and remaining ingredients, except bean liquid. Heat and add the bean liquid as needed. Simmer for at least 1 hour.

▶ Bob French's Colorado Chili

ingredients

2 ancho chiles

2 dried Anaheim chiles

1 pound ground turkey

1 cup chicken broth

2 Tbsp. vegetable oil

1 medium onion, chopped

1 stalk celery, chopped

2 fresh jalapeño or serrano chiles, unseeded, minced

15-ounce can tomatoes, chopped

¼ tsp. dried sage

1 tsp. dried oregano

15-ounce can black beans

about 1 tsp. salt

Ground Turkey Chili with Black Beans

MAKES 4 TO 6 SERVINGS

*M*ade with a combination of fresh and dried chiles, this is a hot chili.

● Cut the dried chiles in half and remove the stems and seeds. Put them in a small heat-proof bowl. Pour 1 cup boiling water over the chiles, making sure all parts are immersed. Leave chiles to soak about 30 minutes while you prepare other ingredients.

● Crumble and brown the turkey in a skillet. Drain fat, if needed. Put the turkey in a large saucepan with the chicken broth and simmer. Heat the oil in a skillet and sauté the onion and celery 5 minutes. Add the vegetables, along with the fresh chiles, tomatoes, sage, and oregano. Let the turkey simmer.

● Pour the dried chiles and their soaking water into a blender or food processor. Purée until a thick red sauce forms. Strain the sauce to remove seeds and bits of skin. Discard the solids. Add the sauce to the turkey. Simmer the turkey 15 minutes, adding water or chicken broth if needed. Add the beans and salt to taste, and heat through.

Cheesey Chili Beans

MAKES 4 TO 5 SERVINGS

This is a homey, substantial chili. Melting the cheese in the pot cuts the sharpness of the cheese and mellows the heat of the chili. The chili's spiciness will depend on the amount of cayenne used.

● Heat the oil in a skillet and sauté the onion, celery, and garlic 5 minutes, then remove to large saucepan. Add the chopped tomato, beef stock, and tomato sauce.

● Brown the ground beef in the skillet and add to the vegetable mixture. Stir in the chili powder, cumin, and cayenne.

Simmer about 30 minutes, adding a small amount of water or beef stock if needed. Add the beans and salt, then taste and adjust seasonings, keeping in mind that the cheese will add salt. Add the cheese and cook, stirring well, just until the cheese is melted and well blended.

ingredients

2 Tbsp. vegetable oil

1 onion, chopped

1 stalk celery, minced

2 cloves garlic, minced

1 medium tomato, peeled and chopped

1 cup beef stock

8-ounce can tomato sauce

1 pound ground beef

1 Tbsp. commercial chili powder

1 tsp. ground cumin

¼–1 tsp. cayenne

15-ounce can kidney beans, drained

about 1 tsp. salt

2 cups sharp Cheddar cheese, grated

ingredients

3 cups dried pink or red beans, picked over and soaked overnight

about ¼ cup vegetable oil

3 medium onions, chopped

8 cloves garlic, minced

1 stalk celery, finely chopped

½ green bell pepper, finely chopped

1 pound hot pork sausage

1 pound pork, coarsely ground

2 pounds beef, coarsely ground

15-ounce can tomatoes, chopped

8-ounce can tomato sauce

2 beef bouillon cubes

⅓ cup Gephardt's chili powder

1–2 Tbsp. hot New Mexico chile powder

1 Tbsp. ground cumin

2 tsp. dried oregano

2 tsp. dried basil

½ tsp. ground allspice

1 tsp. honey

2–4 tsp. salt

Tailgate Chili

MAKES 12 TO 14 SERVINGS

This is a moderately spicy chili that will feed a small crowd. It uses three meats – hot pork sausage, and coarsely ground beef and pork. If you can't get coarsely ground meat from your grocer and don't have the equipment to do it at home, use lean hamburger for the beef, and cube the pork. This is not a sweet or Cincinnati-style chili. The small amount of allspice adds just another note of flavor, while the honey helps tame the bitterness of the chile powder. For a hotter chili, add more New Mexico chile powder.

● Rinse the beans and put them in a large pot. Add enough water to cover the beans by 2 inches. Bring the beans to a boil, reduce heat and simmer.

● Heat 2 tablespoons of the oil in a large skillet and sauté the onion, garlic, celery, and bell pepper 5 minutes. Add to the beans. Cook the pork sausage, chopping large clumps, until lightly browned. Tilt the pan to drain the fat and remove the sausage with a slotted spoon. Add the sausage to beans. Discard fat or use 1 tablespoon to cook the pork.

● Heat 1 tablespoon vegetable oil or sausage fat and cook the pork until lightly browned. Add to the beans. Heat the remaining vegetable oil and brown the beef. (If necessary, cook the beef in two batches.) Add the browned beef to the beans with the remaining ingredients, except salt. Simmer until the beans are tender, about 1½ hours. Taste and adjust seasonings. Add salt to taste.

Olé Molé Pork Chili

MAKES 6 TO 8 SERVINGS

This is a moderately hot chili that uses the relatively new "hot" or "Mexican" chili powder, available in most supermarket spice sections. Hot chili powder is a mix of ground chiles and other spices, but is hotter than traditional chili powder. This is a meaty chili in a rich sauce. The secret ingredient is molé paste, available in Mexican groceries and some well-stocked supermarkets.

● Drain, rinse and drain the beans. Put them in a large pot and cover with water. Bring to a boil, reduce heat and simmer.

● Heat 1 tablespoon of the oil in a large skillet and cook the pork until browned. Remove the pork with a slotted spoon and add to the beans. Discard the greasy cooking liquids. Heat the remaining oil in the skillet and sauté the onion and garlic 5 minutes, then add to the beans. Add the remaining ingredients, except salt. Cook until the meat and beans are tender, 1½ to 2 hours. Add salt, taste, and adjust seasonings.

ingredients

1 cup black beans, picked over and soaked overnight

2 Tbsp. vegetable oil

2 pounds pork, cubed

1½ medium onions, chopped

2 cloves garlic, minced

1 beef bouillon cube

8-ounce can tomato sauce

1 Tbsp. hot or Mexican chili powder

2 Tbsp. commercial chili powder

2 tsp. dried oregano

1 tsp. celery salt

1 tsp. molé paste

about 1 tsp. salt

Easy Salsa Chili

MAKES 4 TO 6 SERVINGS

This is a quick and easy chili, made with bottled salsa and dried onions. Use the salsa of your choice – it will determine how hot the chili is. To make the chili hotter, add ½ teaspoon or more of Tabasco or other hot pepper sauce.

● Soak the onion flakes in ½ cup water. Brown the meat in a skillet and drain off excess fat. Add the salsa, chili powder, cumin, oregano, and garlic powder to the meat, stir well. Add the onion and soaking water. Simmer the mixture 10 to 15 minutes, until the chili is soupy but not watery. Drain the beans, reserving the liquid. Add the beans to the chili, then add bean liquid as needed. Heat 5 minutes. Add salt, taste, and adjust seasonings.

ingredients

2 Tbsp. dried onion flakes

1 pound ground beef

16-ounce bottle red salsa (about 2 cups)

1 Tbsp. commercial chili powder

1 tsp. ground cumin

1 tsp. dried oregano

½ tsp. garlic powder

15-ounce can kidney beans

about ½ tsp. salt

Chorizo and Black Bean Chili

ingredients

2 cups black beans, picked over and soaked overnight

2 cups beef stock

2 Tbsp. vegetable oil

1 cup chopped onion

1 small green bell pepper, diced

2 cloves garlic, minced

6-ounce can tomato paste

2 Tbsp. commercial chili powder

¼ tsp. cayenne

1 tsp. ground cumin

1 tsp. dried oregano

1 pound chorizo sausage (not smoked)

½ cup green onion, chopped

¼ cup fresh cilantro, chopped

1 cup Monterey jack cheese, grated

1–2 tsp. salt

This chili stretches a pound of chorizo sausage into a substantial meal for six to eight people. It is a moderately spicy chili of complex flavor – the nutty flavor of black beans, the Spanish sausage of pork and paprika, a mix of fresh jalapeños with cayenne and chili powder, plus the mellowing influence of jack cheese. The last-minute addition of green onions and fresh cilantro adds texture. With ¼ teaspoon cayenne, it is moderately spicy – add more for a hotter chili.

● Drain, rinse and drain the beans. Put them in a large pot and cover with water. Add the beef stock, bring to a boil, reduce heat and simmer.

● Heat the oil in a skillet and sauté the onion, bell pepper, and garlic 5 minutes. Add to the beans. Add the tomato paste and seasonings. Continue to let the beans simmer, adding water or stock if needed.

● When the beans have cooked about 1 hour, crumble the chorizo into a skillet. Fry until the meat is cooked and the fat is rendered out. With a slotted spoon remove the meat – taking care to drain the fat – and add it to the beans. Discard the fat.

● Continue simmering the beans until tender, 1½ to 2 hours. Five minutes before serving, add the green onion and cilantro. Add salt, taste, and adjust seasonings. Immediately before serving, stir in the cheese, so it is only partially melted when served.

Smokin' Chipotle Turkey Chili

MAKES 4 TO 6 SERVINGS

This is a hot chili stew with the delicious, smoky flavor of chipotle chiles. If you have leftover turkey from a holiday bird, no one will complain about being served turkey yet another time. Add a third chipotle chile for a really hot dish. If you cannot find Rotel tomatoes, use regular canned tomatoes plus one chopped Anaheim chile, canned or fresh.

● Heat the oil in a skillet and sauté the garlic and onion 5 minutes. Put the vegetables in a large saucepan with the chicken broth and turkey. Bring to a boil. Add the remaining ingredients, except the beans and salt. Reduce the heat and simmer at least 30 minutes, up to 1 hour, adding water or chicken broth if needed. Add the beans. Taste, add salt, and adjust seasonings.

ingredients

2 Tbsp. vegetable oil

3 cloves garlic, minced

1 medium onion, chopped

2 cups chicken broth

2 cups cubed cooked turkey

2–3 minced chipotle chiles

10-ounce can Rotel diced tomatoes with green chiles

8-ounce can tomato sauce

3 Tbsp. chili powder

1 tsp. ground cumin

1 tsp. celery salt

1 tsp. ground coriander

1 tsp. unsweetened cocoa

16-ounce can pinto or red beans

about ½ tsp. salt

Chili with Ground Beef and Hot Italian Sausage

MAKES 6 SERVINGS

This is a moderately hot chili, accented by the flavors of the Italian sausage.

● Drain, rinse and drain the beans. Put them in a large saucepan and add water to cover by 2 inches. Bring to a boil, reduce heat and simmer.

● Crumble the ground beef and sausage into a large skillet and cook until browned. Remove the meat and add to the beans. Discard the fat, or, if it is not watery, save 2 tablespoons for sautéing the vegetables and discard the rest.

● Reheat the sausage fat or heat the vegetable oil and sauté the onion, celery, and garlic 5 minutes. Add to the beans with the remaining ingredients, except salt. Simmer until the beans are tender, a total of at least 1½ hours, adding water if needed. When the beans are tender, add salt, taste, and adjust seasonings.

ingredients

1 cup dried pinto beans, picked over and soaked overnight

1 pound ground beef

8 ounces hot Italian-style sausage

2 Tbsp. vegetable oil, if needed

1 onion, chopped

1 stalk celery, chopped

2 cloves garlic, minced

2 Tbsp. commercial chili powder

1 tsp. dried oregano

1 tsp. dried basil

½ tsp. cayenne

4-ounce can chopped green chiles

8-ounce can tomato sauce

about 1 tsp. salt

Double Turkey Chili with Green Chiles

ingredients

- 6 large Anaheim chiles
- 1 Tbsp. vegetable oil
- 1 pound uncooked turkey meat, cubed
- 6 ounces turkey sausage
- 1 medium onion, chopped
- 1 stalk celery, finely chopped
- 2 cloves garlic, minced
- 3 cups chicken stock
- 15-ounce can tomatoes
- ½ tsp. cayenne or to taste
- 15-ounce can white or kidney beans
- 1–2 tsp. salt

*T*urkey and turkey sausage can provide a lower-cholesterol alternative to traditional beef and pork chilis. Check the turkey sausage, however, as some products include a high percentage of turkey fat and skin. Any part of the turkey can provide the cubed turkey. The easiest but priciest alternative is using turkey cutlets. This is a substantial chili with a savory, moderately spicy sauce. It is made with mild green Anaheim chiles, and the heat is provided by cayenne, but other green chiles can be substituted.

● Roast the chiles under a broiler, turning, until skin on all sides is blistered and mostly blackened. Put the chiles in a paper bag or covered bowl to steam.

● Heat the oil in a large skillet, add the turkey meat and crumble in the turkey sausage. Cook until browned. Add the onion, celery, and garlic, and cook 5 minutes. Put the meat and vegetables in a large saucepan with the chicken stock. Bring to a boil, reduce heat and simmer.

● Peel the blackened skins from the chiles and remove the stems and seeds. Chop half the chiles and add to the stew. Cut the three remaining chiles in several large pieces. Put the chiles and tomatoes in a blender or food processor with as much of the tomato liquid as is needed and purée. Add the tomato-chile purée, and any remaining tomato liquid, to the chili. Add the cayenne.

● When the chili has simmered at least 45 minutes, add the beans and cook 5 minutes. Add the salt, taste, and adjust seasonings.

Pork Chili with Italian Sausage

*F*ennel in the Italian sausage adds a pleasing accent to this moderately hot chili.

ingredients

1 pound ground pork

4 ounces Italian sausage

1 Tbsp. vegetable oil

1 onion, chopped

2 cloves garlic, minced

6-ounce can tomato paste

2 Tbsp. commercial chili powder

1 Tbsp. hot New Mexico chile powder

1 tsp. dried oregano

1 tsp. ground cumin

1 Tbsp. lime juice

16-ounce can pinto beans

about 1 tsp. salt

● Brown the pork and sausage in a hot skillet. Drain off excess fat. Put the meat in a large saucepan and set aside. Heat the oil in the skillet and sauté the onion and garlic 5 minutes. Add to the meat with 2 cups water, the tomato paste, and seasonings. Mix well and bring to a boil. Reduce heat and simmer about 1 hour and 15 minutes. Add the lime juice and beans. Simmer 15 minutes. Add salt, taste, and adjust seasonings.

Pork and Black Bean Chili with Tomatillos

*T*his is a pleasantly spicy, slightly tart chili that uses tomatillos instead of tomato sauce. If fresh tomatillos are not available, substitute canned ones, which do not have to be boiled before using.

ingredients

1 cup dry black beans, picked over and soaked overnight

2 Tbsp. vegetable oil

2 pounds pork, cubed

1 large onion, chopped

1 pound tomatillos

2 tsp. chicken bouillon

1 tsp. garlic powder

2 Tbsp. commercial chili powder

1 Tbsp. hot New Mexico chile powder

1 tsp. ground cumin

1 tsp. dried marjoram

1–2 tsp. salt

● Drain the beans, put in a large pot and add enough water to cover by 2 inches. Bring to a boil, reduce heat and simmer.
● Heat 1 tablespoon of the oil in a large, deep skillet or big saucepan and cook the pork until lightly browned. Add the pork to the beans. Heat the remaining oil in the skillet and sauté the onion 5 minutes. Add the onion to the beans.
● Boil water in a medium saucepan. Husk and rinse the tomatillos, then add them to the boiling water. Simmer the tomatillos until they are soft, 10 to 15 minutes. Remove the tomatillos and drain them. Purée the tomatillos in a blender or food processor. Add the purée to the chili. Add the bouillon and spices to the chili. Continue simmering the chili until the pork has cooked about 1½ hours, adding water if needed. Add salt, taste, and adjust seasonings.

Venison Chili with Nopalitos

MAKES 5 TO 6 SERVINGS

Because it is very lean, even ground venison needs to be cooked with added fat. The bacon drippings provide extra flavor, but olive oil can be substituted. Venison's strong flavor stands up nicely to hot chiles. Nopalitos, bits of cactus, add flavor reminiscent of green beans. Canned or bottled nopalitos are available in the Mexican section of many grocery stores. This chili is moderately spicy.

● In a large, wide pot, heat the bacon drippings and sauté the onion, bell pepper, and garlic 5 minutes. Add the venison and cook until lightly browned. Add the beer, 2 cups water, and tomato sauce. Stir well, bring to a boil, reduce heat. Mix in the seasonings and simmer 1 hour. Add the nopalitos and beans. Simmer 20 minutes. Add salt, taste, and adjust seasonings.

ingredients

3 Tbsp. bacon drippings

1 onion, chopped

½ green bell pepper, finely chopped

3 cloves garlic, minced

1½ pounds coarsely ground venison

1½ cups beer

8-ounce can tomato sauce

2 Tbsp. commercial chili powder

2 Tbsp. hot or Mexican commercial chili powder

1 tsp. ground cumin

1 tsp. dried marjoram

¼ tsp. dried thyme

11-ounce jar nopalitos, rinsed, drained and chopped

15-ounce can black beans, undrained

1 tsp. salt

Kitchen Sink Chili

This moderately spicy chili has beef, turkey sausage, tomatoes, mushrooms, olives, beans – everything but the kitchen sink.

ingredients

3 pounds ground beef

1 pound turkey sausage

3 onions, chopped

6 cloves garlic, minced

½ green bell pepper, finely chopped

3 cups beef stock

8-ounce can tomato sauce

15-ounce can tomatoes, chopped

¼ cup mild chile molido

1 Tbsp. hot chile powder

1 Tbsp. ground cumin

1 Tbsp. dried oregano

¼ tsp. ground allspice

2 cups mushrooms, sliced

2 × 2¼-ounce cans sliced olives

3 × 16-ounce cans kidney or pinto beans

● Crumble the beef and sausage into a large stockpot. Cook, chopping any large pieces, until browned. Spoon off and discard the fat. Add 2 cups water and the remaining ingredients, except the olives, beans, and salt. Stir well, bring to a boil, then reduce heat. Simmer 1 hour, stirring occasionally and adding water if needed. Add the olives and beans, and simmer 15 minutes. Add some salt, taste, and adjust seasonings.

UNTRADITIONAL CHILIS

If it wasn't bad enough that people spoiled the purity of good chili by adding beans, some cooks went farther. Some cookbooks include chilis made with sauerkraut, raisins, pumpkin, and other truly odd ingredients. For those with an adventurous palate, here are nine chilis that stretch the standard, from Sissy Chili for the Gourmet Palate (sun-dried tomatoes, olives, goat cheese) to Slightly Seedy Chili (toasted sesame and caraway seeds) to that midwestern favorite, Cincinnati Five-Way Chili, seasoned with turmeric, cardamom, and cinnamon, and served over spaghetti.

Slightly Seedy Chili

MAKES 4 TO 6 SERVINGS

ingredients

2 Tbsp. vegetable oil

1 onion, chopped

3 cloves garlic, minced

1 stalk celery, finely chopped

¼ green bell pepper, finely chopped

1 pound ground beef

2 beef bouillon cubes

15-ounce can tomatoes, chopped

8-ounce can tomato sauce

3 Tbsp. commercial chili powder

1 Tbsp. hot New Mexico chile powder

½–1 tsp. crushed red chile flakes

1 tsp. caraway seeds

1 Tbsp. sesame seeds

16-ounce can kidney beans

½–1 tsp. salt

*T*his looks and tastes – at least initially – like a typical chili of moderate heat. But there is a note of nutty flavor with just the faintest hint of sweetness, added by the toasted sesame and caraway seeds, which are not quite recognizable.

● Heat the oil in a skillet and sauté the onion, garlic, celery, and bell pepper 5 minutes. Put vegetables in a large saucepan and set aside. Add the beef to the skillet and cook until browned. Drain off fat and add the beef to the saucepan with the vegetables. Dissolve the bouillon cubes in 1 cup boiling water. Add to the beef with 2 more cups water. Stir and bring to a boil. Add the tomatoes, tomato sauce, chili powders, and chile flakes. Mix well, reduce heat and simmer.

● Put the caraway and sesame seeds in a small, dry skillet over medium heat. Toast the seeds, shaking frequently so they don't scorch, until the sesame seeds are golden. Add to the chili. After chili has simmered about 1 hour, add the beans, plus liquid if needed. Taste, add salt, and adjust seasonings.

Sissy Chili for the Gourmet Palate

MAKES 4 SERVINGS

*I*ngredients in this mildly spicy chili are a bit unusual – goat cheese, sun-dried tomatoes, and black olives. A chili-lover with an asbestos palate would scorn it as something for sissies, but it's truly delicious. Sun-dried tomatoes give it a bit of tang and an interesting texture, olives add a touch of sweetness, and the strong flavor of goat cheese balances the spicy flavor. For a somewhat hotter chili, don't remove the jalapeños' seeds and veins. It is easier to cut the sun-dried tomatoes with kitchen shears than it is to chop them. And remember that the pieces will swell as they absorb cooking liquids.

● Heat 1 tablespoon of the oil in a large skillet and sauté the onion and garlic 5 minutes. Heat the remaining oil in the skillet and cook the beef until lightly browned. Put the vegetables and beef in a saucepan. Add the beef stock, 2 cups water, tomato sauce, and seasonings.

Bring to a boil, reduce heat and simmer 1 hour.

● Add the sun-dried tomatoes and jalapeños. Simmer 30 minutes. Add the olives, cilantro, and salt, taste, and adjust seasonings. Ladle into bowls and sprinkle the goat cheese over the chili.

ingredients

2 Tbsp. olive oil

1 medium onion, chopped

4 cloves garlic, minced

2 pounds beef, cubed

2 cups beef stock

8-ounce can tomato sauce

2 Tbsp. commercial chili powder

1 tsp. dried oregano

1 tsp. dried basil

¼ tsp. dried rosemary, crushed

½ cup sun-dried tomatoes, coarsely chopped

2 jalapeño chiles, seeded and minced

2¼-ounce can sliced olives

3 Tbsp. fresh cilantro, chopped

about ½ tsp. salt

2–3 ounces goat cheese, crumbled

Garlicky Pork Chili

ingredients

16 cloves garlic

about 4 Tbsp. olive oil

1 cup dry black beans, picked over and soaked overnight

2 cups chicken stock

1 medium onion, chopped

2 pounds pork, diced

1 tsp. ground cumin

1 tsp. paprika

1 tsp. dried oregano

8-ounce can tomato sauce

1 Tbsp. mild New Mexico chile powder

1 Tbsp. ancho chile powder

about 1 tsp. salt

*M*ild New Mexico and moderate ancho chile powders provide the background for the delicious garlic flavor of this pork and black bean chili. California chile powder can substitute if you can't find mild New Mexico chile powder.

● Preheat the oven to 350°F. Put 8 of the garlic cloves on a square of foil about 8 by 8 inches. Brush with 1 tablespoon of the olive oil. Wrap the foil around the garlic to form a sealed bundle. Bake 35 minutes. Remove from the oven, open the foil and let cool.

● Drain the beans. Put in a large pot, add just enough water to cover, then add the chicken stock. Bring to a boil, reduce heat and simmer.

● Heat 1 tablespoon of the oil in a skillet and sauté the onion 5 minutes. Add to the beans. Add another 1 tablespoon of the oil to the skillet and brown the pork. Add to the beans.

● Mince the remaining 8 cloves garlic. Heat the remaining oil in very small skillet and cook the minced garlic, cumin, paprika and oregano, stirring often, 1 minute. Add to the beans.

● Squeeze the roasted garlic from the papery peel. Add to the beans with the tomato sauce and chile powders. Stir well and continue cooking until the beans and pork are tender, about 1½ hours. Add salt, taste, and adjust seasonings.

Fried Chicken Chili

MAKES 4 TO 6 SERVINGS

*C*ubes of chicken are coated with spices, then fried before being added to the chili broth, giving the meat extra spice. This is a hot chili that gets balance from the pinto beans.

● Mix the flour with the cayenne, chili powder, cumin, oregano, garlic powder, and salt. Put the mixture in a bag. Add the chicken and shake until the chicken cubes are evenly coated with spice mixture.

● Heat 2 tablespoons of the oil in a large skillet and cook the chicken, turning as needed, until the chicken is lightly browned on all sides. Set the chicken aside. Heat the remaining oil in the skillet and sauté the onion 5 minutes.

● Put the chicken and onion in a large saucepan with the chicken broth. Add the remaining ingredients, except the beans and salt. Bring to a boil, reduce heat and simmer about 1 hour, adding water if needed. Add the beans. Taste, add salt, and adjust seasonings.

ingredients

2 Tbsp. flour

¼ tsp. cayenne

1 tsp. chili powder

½ tsp. ground cumin

½ tsp. dried oregano

½ tsp. garlic powder

¼ tsp. salt

4 chicken half-breasts, cubed

3 Tbsp. vegetable oil

1 onion, chopped

2 cups chicken broth

¼ cup commercial chili powder

1 Tbsp. hot New Mexico chile powder

1 tsp. ground cumin

1 tsp. dried oregano

20-ounce can pinto beans

about 1 tsp. salt

Cincinnati Five-way Chili

MAKES 6 TO 8 SERVINGS

ingredients

2 pounds ground beef

1½ onions, chopped

2 cloves garlic, minced

1 Tbsp. red wine vinegar

1 tsp. cinnamon

½ tsp. allspice

¼ tsp. ground cloves

¼ tsp. ground cardamom

1 tsp. dried oregano

½ tsp. ground cumin

¼ tsp. turmeric (can substitute curry powder)

2 Tbsp. commercial chili powder

½ tsp. crushed chili flakes, or more to taste (optional)

6-ounce can tomato paste

about 1 tsp. salt

15-ounce can kidney beans

1 pound spaghetti, cooked

2 cups (about 8 ounces) Cheddar cheese, grated

1½ onions, chopped (for layer)

*S*ometimes called chili-mac, Cincinnati Chili is a Texas purist's nightmare. Not only does it come with tomatoes and beans, but is served on top of spaghetti! There's a bit of eastern Mediterranean influence in the spices, which are truly a potpourri – cinnamon, cloves, cardamom, turmeric, cumin, and oregano, in addition to the chili powder. Typically it's not as hot as more traditional chilis. It's a layered chili, with the five layers – spaghetti, chili, beans, chopped onion, and grated Cheddar cheese – accounting for its name. But among midwesterners,. Cincinnati Chili has as many devotees as Texas chili does in the Southwest. In this version, optional crushed chile flakes add the heat.

● In a large pot, brown the ground beef. Add the onion and garlic and cook 5 minutes. Spoon off any excess fat. Add 3 cups water, the vinegar, spices and herbs, chili flakes, and tomato paste. Mix well. Bring to a boil, reduce heat and simmer 2 hours, stirring occasionally and adding water if needed. Just before serving, add salt, taste, and adjust seasonings.

● You can heat the kidney beans and serve them on the side, or mix them with the chili before serving. To serve, begin with a layer of spaghetti, add the chili, then the beans, cheese, and onion.

California Five-way Chili

MAKES 6 TO 8 SERVINGS

*T*his variation of Cincinnati chili uses Mexican ingredients that have become staples in California kitchens: chorizo sausage, black beans, cilantro, and a combination of unsweetened cocoa, cinnamon, and cloves that are reminiscent of mole dishes. It is pleasantly spicy.

● Brown the ground beef in a skillet. Spoon off the excess fat, put the meat in large pot and set aside. Brown the chorizo sausage in a skillet. Drain off all but 1 tablespoon of the fat, and remove the sausage with a slotted spoon. Add the sausage to the pot. Reheat the fat and sauté the onion and garlic 5 minutes. Add to the pot.

● Add the cocoa and seasonings to the pot. Add the vinegar and tomato paste and 2 cups water. Bring the mixture to a boil, stirring well. Reduce heat and simmer about 1 hour and 15 minutes, adding water if necessary. Add the cilantro and salt to taste.

● Traditionally, the beans are one of the five layers in five-way chili, but if you wish to mix the beans into the chili, do so now.

● To serve, start with a layer of spaghetti, add the chili, beans, chopped onion, and cheese.

ingredients

1½ pounds ground beef

8 ounces chorizo sausage (not smoked)

1 onion, chopped

3 cloves garlic, minced

2 tsp. unsweetened cocoa

1 tsp. cinnamon

¼ tsp. ground cloves

1 tsp. ground cumin

1 tsp. dried oregano

2 Tbsp. commercial chili powder

1 Tbsp. hot or Mexican commercial chili powder

1 Tbsp. red wine vinegar

6-ounce can tomato paste

¼ cup fresh cilantro, chopped

about 1 tsp. salt

16-ounce can black beans

¾ pound spaghetti, cooked

1½ onions, chopped (for layer)

8 ounces Cheddar cheese, grated

◀ *California Five-Way Chili*

Smoked Turkey Chili

MAKES 6 SERVINGS

S moked turkey is like ham — with beans, it doesn't take a large amount to make this chili a meaty dish. It is a little soupy. The heat will depend on the type of dried chiles you use, but the smoked turkey stands up well to hot chiles. I like a combination of two New Mexico, two Anaheim, and two chiles negroes, which makes a moderately hot chili. Frijoles colorados are small red beans. One large turkey drumstick will produce nearly 2 cups of chopped meat.

ingredients

2 cups frijoles colorados, picked over and soaked overnight

6 large dried chiles

2 Tbsp. vegetable oil

1½ medium onions, chopped

2 stalks celery, chopped

1½–2 cups smoked turkey, shredded or chopped

15-ounce can tomatoes, chopped

2 chicken bouillon cubes

2 tsp. dried oregano

1 tsp. ground cumin

1 tsp. celery salt

1 tsp. garlic powder

½ tsp. sugar

½–1 tsp. salt

● Drain, rinse and drain the beans. Put them in a large pot and cover them with water. Bring to a boil, reduce heat and simmer.

● Cut the dried chiles in half and remove the stems and seeds. Place the chiles in a small, heat-proof bowl and pour 1 cup boiling water over. Let them soak 30 minutes, making sure that all the pieces of chile are covered with water.

● While the chiles are soaking, heat the oil in a skillet and sauté the onion and celery 5 minutes, then add to the beans. Add the turkey, chopped tomatoes, crumbled bouillon, oregano, cumin, celery salt, garlic powder, and sugar to the beans.

● Put the chiles and their soaking water in a blender or food processor. Purée until a smooth red-brown sauce forms. Strain the sauce to remove seeds and bits of skin, discard the solids. Add the sauce to the beans.

● Simmer the chili, adding water if needed, until the beans are tender, at least 1½ hours. Add salt, taste, and adjust seasonings.

◄ *Smoked Turkey Chili*

Marinated Chicken Chili with Mushrooms and Green Chiles

MAKES 4 TO 5 SERVINGS

T*his is a mild chili, made with chicken that has been marinated in a spicy vinaigrette.*

● Combine the vinaigrette, 2 cloves garlic, cilantro, and cumin, and shake well. Put the chicken in a sealable plastic bag or a plastic bowl with a lid. Pour the vinaigrette over the chicken and stir well so all pieces are coated. Let chicken marinate in the refrigerator at least 2 hours or as long as overnight.

● Heat 1 tablespoon of the oil in a skillet and sauté the onion and remaining garlic 5 minutes. Put in a large saucepan with the chicken stock, oregano, and 1 cup water. Heat another tablespoon oil in the skillet. Drain and discard the excess marinade from the chicken. Sauté the chicken cubes until lightly browned. Add to the chicken stock. Bring to a boil, reduce heat and simmer.

● Roast the chiles under the broiler, turning often until they are charred on all sides. Remove from the broiler and put in a bag. Close the bag and let the chiles steam at least 10 minutes. Remove them from the bag, cut off and discard the stems and seeds. Peel and discard the blackened skin. Put half the chiles in blender or food processor with a little liquid from the pot and purée. Add the purée to the pot. Chop the remaining chiles and add them to the pot.

● Heat the remaining 2 tablespoons oil and sauté the mushrooms 10 minutes. Add them to the chili. After the chicken has simmered 1 hour, add salt, taste, and adjust seasonings.

ingredients

⅓ cup bottled vinaigrette

3 cloves garlic, minced

2 Tbsp. fresh cilantro, chopped

½ tsp. ground cumin

4 chicken half-breasts, cubed

4 Tbsp. olive oil

1 medium onion, chopped

2 cups chicken stock

1 tsp. dried oregano

6 poblano chiles, or 3 poblanos and 3 Anaheims

2 cups mushrooms, sliced

about 1 tsp. salt

ALIAS CHILI

It is hard to draw the line between what is a chili and what's not. As long as we are defining chili liberally, here are six stews of meat and chile that are known by other names, but could be considered chilis as well. They range from Feijoada, a garlicky Brazilian stew of pork and black beans, to Bredie, a South African stew of mutton, tomato juice, and beans.

Feijoada

ingredients

2 cups dry black beans, picked over and soaked overnight

4 Tbsp. vegetable oil

3 dried chiles de arbol, whole

8 cloves garlic, minced

2 pounds pork loin, cubed

1 large onion, chopped

15-ounce can tomatoes, chopped

1 pound linguica, cut into ¼-inch slices

3 jalapeño chiles, unseeded, minced

about 2 tsp. salt

Feijoada, a spicy stew of black beans and pork, is the ceremonial dish of Brazil. Traditionally it is made with various parts of the pig, such as snout, ears, tail, and feet. This hot Americanized version uses pork loin and linguica, a garlicky Portuguese sausage. Serve Feijoada with rice, greens, and orange slices. If you cannot find chiles de arbol, any small hot dried red chiles will do.

● Drain the beans, put them in a stockpot and add enough water to cover by 2 inches. Bring to a boil, reduce heat and simmer.

● Heat 1 tablespoon of the oil in a small skillet and sauté the chiles de arbol and half the minced garlic 1 to 2 minutes, until the garlic just starts to brown. Add to the beans. Heat another 1 tablespoon oil in a large skillet and cook the pork until lightly browned. Add the pork to the beans. Heat the remaining 2 tablespoons oil in a skillet and sauté the onion and remaining half of the minced garlic 5 minutes, then add to the beans.

● Add the tomatoes and linguica to the beans. Return the stew to a boil, reduce heat and simmer. When beans have simmered 1 hour, add the jalapeños. Continue simmering until the beans are tender, a total of 1½ to 2 hours. Add salt, taste, and adjust seasonings.

◄ *Feijoada*

Carnitas Chili

MAKES 4 SERVINGS

Carnitas, a Mexican dish, are little chunks of meat served with a hot sauce for dipping, or shredded, mixed with sauce and used as a filling for enchiladas. This hot version mixes the shredded twice-cooked meat and sauce to make a chili-like stew. Serve it with rice or warm tortillas.

● Combine the chili powder, cumin, oregano, garlic, and onion powders. Put in a bag with the pork chunks. Shake until the meat is evenly covered, then use your fingers to rub it in. Let the meat sit at room temperature 45 minutes to absorb the spice flavors. Heat 2 tablespoons of the oil in a Dutch oven or other large, oven-proof pot and brown the meat on all sides, turning often so the spices do not scorch. Add the onion pieces and enough water to cover the meat. Bring to a boil, reduce heat and simmer, covered, 1½ hours. Preheat the oven to 350°F. Put the pot of meat in the oven and bake, uncovered, 45 minutes.

● While the meat is in the oven, prepare the chiles. Remove the stems and seeds and cut each chile into 4 pieces. Put the chiles in a narrow deep bowl. Boil the beef stock and pour over the chiles. Stir so all pieces are soaking. Let the chiles soak 30 minutes. Meanwhile, heat the remaining oil in a skillet and sauté the onion 10 minutes. Set aside. Pour the chiles and their soaking liquid into a blender or food processor. Purée until a smooth sauce forms. Strain to remove seeds and the bits of skin, discard the solids. Combine the sauce with the sautéed onion.

● When the meat has cooked 45 minutes, remove from the oven. Pour any remaining liquids into the chile sauce. Let meat sit until it is cool enough to handle. Shred the meat. Heat the chile sauce and stir in the meat. Add salt to taste.

ingredients

1 Tbsp. commercial chili powder

2 tsp. ground cumin

2 tsp. dried oregano

1 tsp. garlic powder

1 tsp. onion powder

2 pounds pork loin, cut into 8 or 10 chunks

3 Tbsp. vegetable oil

1 onion, cut into eighths

6 large dried red chiles, preferably New Mexico or chiles negros or a combination

1 cup beef stock

1 medium onion, chopped

about 1 tsp. salt

ingredients

2 lamb shanks

2 bay leaves

1 cup dry pinto beans, picked over and soaked overnight

2 Tbsp. vegetable oil

1 large onion, chopped

2 cloves garlic, minced

1 tsp. fresh ginger, grated

1 tsp. ground coriander

¼ tsp. ground cardamom

1 tsp. fennel seed

½ tsp. dried thyme

1 tsp. dried oregano

2 Tbsp. commercial chili powder

2 cups tomato juice

6-ounce can tomato paste

1–2 tsp. salt

Tabasco sauce to taste

Bredie

Bredie is a South African stew of mutton, tomato juice, and dried spotted beans similar to pinto beans. Its exotic combination of seasonings — cardamom, fennel, and ginger — also includes some form of chiles. This version, made with lamb shanks, is mildly spicy, but can be made hotter with Tabasco sauce.

● Put the lamb shanks and bay leaves in a stockpot and cover with water. Bring to a boil, reduce heat and simmer 45 minutes. Drain the beans and add to the lamb. Add enough water to cover by 1 inch. Return to a boil, reduce heat and simmer 30 minutes. Remove the lamb shanks and let cool slightly while you prepare the other ingredients.

● Heat the oil in a large skillet and sauté the onion and garlic 2 minutes. Add the ginger, coriander, cardamom, fennel seed, thyme, and oregano, sauté 5 minutes longer. Add to the beans. Add the chili powder, tomato juice, and tomato paste to the beans. Return to a boil, reduce heat and continue simmering, stirring occasionally and adding water if needed.

● When the lamb has cooled enough to handle, cut the meat and fat from the bones. Discard the fat and bones. Shred the meat and add it to the beans. When the beans are tender — about 1½ hours total cooking time — add salt and Tabasco to taste.

Michelle's Green Chile Stew with Pork

MAKES 6 SERVINGS

Michelle Murray and I grew up baking chocolate chip cookies together in Los Angeles. Later, I moved to Florida and Michelle moved to New Mexico, where she makes this delicious baked stew of pork, potatoes, and roasted green chiles. The stew's heat depends on the type of green chiles used. For a hot dish, add several unseeded jalapeños or serrano chiles.

● Roast the chiles under the broiler, turning, until all sides are blistered and charred but not yet solidly black. Remove the chiles and seal them in a paper bag or a covered dish. Let the chiles steam while you prepare the stew.

● Preheat the oven to 350°F. In a dutch oven or large oven-safe pot, heat 2 tablespoons of the oil. Add the pork and cook, turning occasionally, until the meat is browned on all sides. Remove the pork with a slotted spoon and set aside. Discard liquids. Add the remaining 2 tablespoons oil to the pot and sauté the onion and garlic 5 minutes. Put the pork back in the pan with the herbs, salt, broth, tomato sauce, and tomatoes. Bring to a boil, cover and place in the oven.

● Peel, seed and chop the roasted green chiles. Chop the jalapeños or serranos if you are using them. After the stew has baked 30 minutes, add the chiles and potatoes. Cover and return to the oven. Cook until the meat is tender and potatoes are done, about 1 hour. There should be ample broth, but check once or twice during baking, and add beef stock if needed.

ingredients

8 Anaheim, poblano, or green New Mexico chiles, or a combination

4 Tbsp. vegetable oil

2 pounds pork, cut into 1½-inch chunks

1½ medium onions, chopped

3 cloves garlic, minced

2 tsp. dried oregano

½ tsp. dried rosemary

1 tsp. salt

3 cups beef broth

8-ounce can tomato sauce

15-ounce can tomatoes, chopped

2–3 jalapeño or serrano chiles, unseeded and minced, optional

3–4 medium potatoes, peeled and cut into 1-inch chunks

Hoppin' John with Smoked Turkey

MAKES 6 TO 8 SERVINGS

ingredients

2 cups dried black-eyed peas, picked over and soaked overnight

1 cup smoked turkey, chopped

1 Tbsp. commercial chili powder

1 tsp. ground cumin

2 Tbsp, olive oil

1 large onion, chopped

1 stalk celery, chopped

3 cloves garlic, minced

3 jalapeño chiles, unseeded and minced

2 medium tomatoes, seeded and chopped

4 green onions, chopped

2 Tbsp. fresh cilantro, chopped

about 2 tsp. salt

4 cups cooked white rice

Hoppin' John is spicy black-eyed peas served over rice. It is a Southern dish traditionally eaten on New Year's Day, when it is supposed to bring good luck for the coming year. It is usually flavored with pork, but this recipe uses smoked turkey and lots of chile. If a turkey bone is available, throw it into the pot while the beans are simmering.

● Drain the black-eyed peas, put them in a stockpot and add enough water to cover by 2 inches. Add the turkey meat and, if available, a turkey bone. Add the chili powder and cumin and bring to a boil, reduce heat and simmer.

● Heat the olive oil in a skillet and sauté the onion, celery, garlic, and one of the minced jalapeños 5 minutes, then add to the peas. Continue simmering until the peas are tender, about 1½ hours.

● When the peas are tender, add the remaining jalapeños, the tomatoes, green onions, and cilantro. Add salt, taste, and adjust seasonings. Simmer 2 minutes, then ladle over the bowls of white rice.

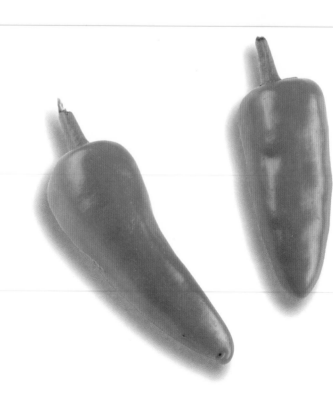

Pozole

Pozole, a main-dish stew of pork, hominy, and chiles, originated in the Mexican state of Jalisco and was adopted by the American Indians of the Southwest. This version begins with a homemade stock of pork and chicken. Pozole is usually eaten with shredded lettuce and chopped radishes and cucumber.

● Put the onion, garlic, celery, pork bones, and chicken parts in a large stockpot and add 3–4 quarts water. Bring to a boil, then reduce heat and simmer, uncovered, for 2 hours. Pour through a wire strainer, skim fat, and return the broth to the heat. You should have at least 2 quarts broth. If not, add enough water to equal 2 quarts. When the bones have cooled slightly, remove any meat and add it back to the broth. Discard the fat, bones, and strained solids.

● Heat the oil in a large saucepan and cook the cubed pork until lightly browned. Add the pork to the broth.

● Remove the stems and seeds from the dried chiles. Cut each chile in several pieces and put in a narrow, deep bowl. Pour 1 cup boiling water over the chiles and let sit for 30 minutes. Purée the chiles and soaking liquid in a blender or food processor to form a smooth sauce. Strain the sauce and discard the solids. Add the sauce to the pork.

● Add the oregano and cumin to the stew. When the pork has simmered at least 1 hour, add the hominy and cilantro. Cook 15 minutes. Add salt, taste, and adjust seasonings.

ingredients

- **1 large onion, cut into chunks**
- **3 cloves garlic, minced**
- **1 stalk celery, cut into several pieces**
- **2 pounds pork neck bones**
- **2 pounds chicken backs, necks, wings**
- **3 Tbsp. vegetable oil**
- **3 pounds pork, cubed**
- **6 large dried chiles, such as ancho or New Mexico**
- **2 tsp. dried oregano**
- **2 tsp. ground cumin**
- **4 cups canned hominy**
- **2 Tbsp. fresh cilantro, chopped**
- **1–2 tsp. salt**

VEGETARIAN CHILI

There is no such dish as vegetarian chili. It's an oxymoron. Chili, by definition, has meat as a primary ingredient. But many vegetarians love chili and have spent hours concocting alternatives to the traditional meaty stew. Typically, one or more types of beans are the backbone of a vegetarian chili – and if you're looking for weird chili ingredients, this is where you will find them. Here are seven recipes for vegetarian chili that include tofu, bulgur, goat cheese, peaches, and a startling array of vegetables.

Vegetarian Black Bean Chili

MAKES 6 TO 8 SERVINGS

Two kinds of chiles plus chili powder make this a pleasantly spicy dish, while fresh cilantro and green onions added at the end add texture. Feta cheese sprinkled on top adds a nice finishing touch.

ingredients

2 cups black beans, picked over and soaked

1 bay leaf

2 ancho chiles

2 Tbsp. vegetable oil

3 medium onions, chopped

2 stalks celery, chopped

3 cloves garlic, minced

2 tsp. ground cumin

2 tsp. dried oregano

1 Tbsp. chili powder

28 ounces canned tomatoes, chopped

1 canned chipotle chile, minced

about 2 tsp. salt

⅔ cup green onions, chopped

¼ cup fresh cilantro, chopped

1 Tbsp. balsamic vinegar

about 4 ounces feta cheese, crumbled

● Drain and rinse the beans. Put them in a large pot and cover with fresh water. Add the bay leaf and bring to a boil. Reduce the heat and simmer the beans while you prepare the other ingredients, adding water if needed.

● Remove the stems and seeds from the ancho chiles. Place the anchos in a small, heat-proof bowl, pour ¾ cup boiling water over them and stir so they are covered. Let them soften in the hot water about 30 minutes.

● Heat the oil in a large skillet and sauté the onion and celery until the celery is soft, 6–8 minutes. (Do this in two batches if you don't have a very large skillet.)

Add the garlic, cumin, oregano, and chili powder and sauté 1 minute longer. Add the mixture to the beans.

● Put the softened ancho chiles and their soaking water in a blender or food processor. Add about ⅓ cup of the chopped tomatoes and the chipotle chile. Purée until smooth. Add the chile mixture to the beans along with the rest of the tomatoes. Continue simmering the beans until tender, 1 hour and 15–30 minutes total. Add salt and adjust to taste. Add the green onions, cilantro and vinegar and cook about 2 minutes. Ladle into bowls and sprinkle feta cheese over top.

Robin's Vegetarian Chili with Peaches and Three Beans

MAKES 12 SERVINGS

Robin Benedick isn't a vegetarian, but she's always looking for meatless dishes. In Orlando, Florida, she found a restaurant that made an unusual vegetarian chili sweetened by peaches – this is her version. Although she likes spicy food, she suggests starting with small amounts of cayenne and Tabasco sauce, then adding more if you want a hotter chili. Use the liquid from the canned tomatoes, and some of the liquid from the beans. Robin doesn't add salt to her chili, but you may wish to add salt if the beans are unsalted.

● Put all the ingredients, except the beans, in a stockpot with about 1 cup water and stir well. Bring to a boil, reduce heat and simmer 30 minutes, stirring often to keep the chili from scorching, and adding water if needed.

● After 30 minutes, add the beans and enough liquid for the desired consistency. Simmer 15 minutes more. Taste and adjust seasonings.

ingredients

- **1 red bell pepper, coarsely chopped**
- **2 green bell peppers, coarsely chopped**
- **1 large onion, coarsely chopped**
- **1 peach, peeled and coarsely chopped**
- **28-ounce can tomatoes, coarsely chopped**
- **28-ounce can tomato sauce**
- **1 tsp. Tabasco sauce**
- **¼ tsp. dried thyme**
- **1 tsp. dried oregano**
- **2 tsp. ground cumin, or more to taste**
- **1 Tbsp. commercial chili powder**
- **1 tsp. black pepper**
- **19-ounce can cannellini beans**
- **2 × 16-ounce cans black beans**
- **16-ounce can kidney beans**

Lentil and Vegetable Chili

MAKES 4 TO 6 SERVINGS

ingredients

1 cup dry kidney beans, picked over and soaked overnight

1 bay leaf

1 Tbsp. vegetable oil

1 stalk celery, chopped

1 medium onion, chopped

1 clove garlic, minced

2 tsp. commercial chili powder

½ tsp. dried oregano

½ tsp. dried basil

14½ ounces canned tomatoes, chopped

⅓ cup dry lentils

¾ cup sliced carrots

¾ cup peas, fresh or frozen

about 1 tsp. salt

This vegetable stew combines kidney beans, lentils, peas, and carrots to make a chunky, mildly spicy vegetarian chili.

● Drain the beans, put them in a large saucepan and cover with fresh water. Add the bay leaf. Bring to a boil, reduce heat and simmer. Heat the oil in a skillet and sauté the celery and onion 5 minutes. Add the garlic and sauté 1 minute. Add the vegetables to the beans, along with the chili powder, oregano, basil, and tomatoes. Return to a boil, reduce heat and simmer, adding water if needed.

● After the beans have cooked 1 hour, add the lentils. (Lentil cooking times vary, depending on how they were processed. If the cooking instructions on the package are more or less than 20 minutes, adjust the time you add them to the chili so that they are done about 5 minutes before the chili is ready.) Wait 10 minutes, add water if necessary, then add the carrots. After 5 minutes, add the peas. Cook 10 minutes, add salt and adjust seasonings to taste.

▶ *Lentil and Vegetable Chili*

Angela's Vegetarian Chili

MAKES 6 SERVINGS

ingredients

1 Tbsp. vegetable oil

1 onion, chopped

1 green bell pepper, chopped

2 cloves garlic, minced

1 can Campbell's Tomato Rice Soup

16-ounce can tomatoes, including juice, chopped

6-ounce can tomato paste

16-ounce can corn

4 Tbsp. commercial chili powder

2 × 16-ounce cans kidney beans

ketchup to taste

hot pepper sauce

cayenne

This chili started with a beefy recipe from Campbell's Soup, but Angela Bradbery kept fiddling with it until she got the chili she wanted — no meat, lots of beans and vegetables, not quite so sweet. She uses both hot pepper sauce and cayenne to taste, so the dish is as mild or as spicy as you want.

● Heat the oil in a skillet and sauté the onion, bell pepper, and garlic 5 minutes. Put the vegetables in a large saucepan with the soup, tomatoes, tomato paste, corn and chili powder. Stir well and add 1 cup water or so for a soupy consistency. Add the kidney beans, plus the ketchup, hot pepper sauce, and cayenne to taste. Bring to a boil, reduce heat and simmer 30 minutes.

Vegetarian Chili with Tofu

MAKES 6 SERVINGS

This is a thick, tomatoey chili with fried bits of tofu. Its hotness depends on the type of dried chiles used.

ingredients

12 ounces firm tofu

6 dried Anaheim, ancho, pasilla, or New Mexico chiles, or a combination

about 4 Tbsp. vegetable oil

1 large onion, chopped

1 green bell pepper, chopped

2 stalks celery, chopped

4 cloves garlic, minced

2 cups vegetable broth

8 ounces tomato sauce

15-ounce can tomatoes, chopped

1 tsp. ground cumin

1 tsp. ground coriander

2 tsp. dried oregano

1 tsp. paprika

¼ cup fresh cilantro, chopped

about 1 tsp. salt

● If not using pressed tofu, it should be pressed to remove excess water. Place the tofu on a plate, put another plate on top and weight it with cans or other heavy objects. Tofu should be pressed at least 30 minutes before using.

● Split the dried chiles in half and remove the stems and seeds. Put the pieces in a small heat-proof bowl and pour 1 cup boiling water over the chiles. Let them steep in the water 30 minutes, stirring occasionally to be sure all parts of the chiles are covered with water.

● Heat 2 tablespoons of the oil in a large skillet and sauté the onion, bell pepper, celery, and garlic 5 minutes. Put the sautéed vegetables in a large pot with the broth, tomato sauce, tomatoes, and seasonings. Bring to a boil, reduce heat and simmer.

● After the chiles have soaked for 30 minutes, pour the chiles and the soaking liquid into a blender or food processor. Purée until a smooth sauce is formed. Strain the sauce to remove seeds and bits of skin, discard solids. Add the strained sauce to the simmering sauce.

● Discard the liquids from the tofu. Cut the tofu into ¼-inch cubes. Heat the remaining oil in a skillet and fry the tofu over medium-high, turning once, until tofu is slightly browned, 2 to 3 minutes a side. Add the tofu to the chili. Let the chili simmer 30 minutes. Add the cilantro and salt, taste, and adjust seasonings.

Vegetarian Chili with Corn and Bulgur

MAKES 6 TO 8 SERVINGS

ingredients

1 cup dry kidney beans, picked over and soaked overnight

2 cups vegetable broth

2 Tbsp. vegetable oil

1½ medium onions, chopped

½ green bell pepper, chopped

3 cloves garlic, minced

1 carrot, peeled and coarsely chopped

15-ounce can tomatoes, chopped

6-ounce can tomato paste

2 Tbsp. commercial chili powder

2 Tbsp. hot or Mexican commercial chili powder

1 tsp. ground cumin

1 tsp. dried oregano

⅓ cup bulgur

1 cup corn, fresh or frozen

5-ounce can black olives, sliced

salt to taste

This pleasantly spicy chili, with corn and olives, may remind you of old-fashioned tamale pie. It is thickened with bulgur, a partially cooked cracked wheat available in health-food stores.

● Drain the kidney beans, put in large pot and add just enough water to cover. Add 1 cup of the vegetable broth. Bring to a boil, reduce heat and simmer.

● Heat the oil in a large skillet and sauté the onion, bell pepper, and garlic 5 minutes. Add to the beans with the carrot, tomatoes, tomato paste, and spices. Stir and continue simmering.

● After the beans have simmered about 45 minutes, put the remaining 1 cup vegetable broth in a small pan and bring to a boil. Add the bulgur, stir well, and boil 5 minutes. Remove from the heat and let stand 10 minutes. Add the bulgur and broth to the chili. Add the corn and continue cooking, stirring often and adding water if needed, until the beans are tender, about 30 minutes (about 1½ hours total). Stir in the olives. Taste, add salt if needed, and adjust seasonings.

Three-bean Vegetarian Chili

This mildly spicy chili starts with a base of three beans — black beans, pinquitos, and garbanzos. It gets its flavor from three kinds of chiles and three forms of tomatoes, including sun-dried tomatoes, which provide bits of tart, chewy surprise.

● The night before: pick over the three types of beans for stones or other debris. Put all the beans in a big bowl or pot, fill with water and let soak overnight.

● After the beans have soaked at least 8 hours, drain them, rinse, and drain again. Put them in a large pot and add enough water to cover by 2 inches. Bring to a boil, reduce heat and simmer.

● Heat the oil in a skillet and sauté the onion, celery, and garlic 5 minutes. Add to the beans with the tomatoes and tomato sauce.

● Roast the chiles under the broiler, turning, until all sides are blistered and nearly blackened. Remove from the broiler and put in a paper bag or covered bowl to steam.

● Add the chili powder to the chili. In a small, dry skillet, heat the cumin seeds, oregano, and basil, shaking frequently, until they are toasted. Remove from the heat and let cool slightly. Grind in a grinder or mortar and pestle, or put between two pieces of waxed paper and crush with the end of a rolling pin. Add to the chili.

● Peel the roasted chiles and remove the stems and seeds. Chop the chiles and add them to the chili.

● Simmer, stirring occasionally and adding water if needed, until the beans are tender, 1½ to 2 hours. About 10 minutes before the chili is done, add the chopped jalapeño and salt. Taste and adjust seasonings. Stir in the cilantro immediately before serving.

ingredients

- ⅔ cup dried black beans
- ⅔ cup dried pinquitos
- ⅔ cup dried garbanzo beans (chickpeas)
- 2 Tbsp. vegetable oil
- 1 large onion, chopped
- 2 stalks celery, chopped
- 4 cloves garlic, minced
- 15-ounce can tomatoes, chopped
- 8-ounce can tomato sauce
- 4 Anaheim or poblano chiles, or a combination
- 2 Tbsp. commercial chili powder
- 2 tsp. cumin seeds
- 2 tsp. dried oregano
- 1 tsp. dried basil
- 1 jalapeño chile, unseeded, minced
- 1–2 tsp. salt
- ¼ cup fresh cilantro, chopped

CHILI AS AN
INGREDIENT

You won't hear any of these wine-tasting adjectives — subtle, impudent, delicate — applied to chili. Chili is hearty and powerful. If you find a chili-lover searching for an adjective, it is usually a search for some variation of hot — fiery, incendiary, a killer. Even in small quantities, chili dominates a dish, even then it's delicious. Here are six ways to use chilis as an ingredient, from the sauce on chili dogs to the filling in tamale pie.

Chili for Chili Dogs and Chili Burgers

MAKES 6 SERVINGS

ingredients

- 1 pound ground beef
- 1 small onion, finely chopped
- 2 cloves garlic, minced
- 1 cup canned enchilada sauce
- ½ tsp. ground cumin
- ½ tsp. dried marjoram
- about ½ cup water

Canned enchilada sauce provides the flavoring for this chili, a thick sauce for spooning over hot dogs and hamburgers. The chili's heat will depend on the type of enchilada sauce, but can be made hotter by adding cayenne or hot pepper sauce.

● In a large skillet, brown the meat, chopping it finely as it cooks. Add the onion and garlic and cook 5 minutes. Drain and discard fat. Add the enchilada sauce, cumin, and marjoram. Add sufficient water to make the sauce slightly watery – it will reduce and thicken as it cooks. Cook over low heat about 15 minutes, or until the sauce is of the desired consistency.

Alma Cherry's Chili Sauce

MAKES ABOUT 6 SERVINGS

ingredients

- 1 pound hamburger
- 1 cup ketchup
- 1 small onion, finely chopped
- 2 stalks celery, finely chopped
- ½ tsp. salt
- chili powder to taste

Half a century ago, Alma Cherry was determined to duplicate the chili sauce served at the family's favorite restaurant in southern Indiana. When the cook refused to divulge the secrets of the popular sauce to any of the customers, Alma pestered the local grocer until he told her what supplies the cook bought. Then she experimented with quantities until she was happy with the sauce, which she uses to make chili dogs. The recipe was given to me by her son, Alan, one of my coworkers. It is a mild sauce, with the celery adding a hint of sweetness.

● Cook the hamburger until browned. Spoon off and discard the fat. Add the ketchup and 1 cup water and mix well. Add the onion and celery and cook until soft, about 10 minutes. Add the salt and chili powder to taste. Cook, stirring frequently, until the sauce is thick.

▶ *Chili for Chili Dogs and Chili Burgers*

Chili Pie

MAKES 6 SERVINGS

*A*lso known as Frito Pie, this simple casserole of corn chips, chili, onion, and cheese is a favorite with kids. Use your choice of chili, with or without beans, but it should be a little soupy, not dry. Bake it in a 10-inch springform pan or 2-quart casserole.

ingredients

4 cups chili

3 cups corn chips

½ medium onion, chopped

2 cups Cheddar cheese, grated

● Preheat the oven to 350°F. Heat the chili until it bubbles. Spread about 2 cups of the corn chips in the bottom of the baking pan. Pour the hot chili over the chips. Sprinkle the onions, then the cheese over the chili, then top with the remaining 1 cup chips. Bake 25 minutes.

Tamale Pie

MAKES 6 TO 8 SERVINGS

*T*his homely dish is an all-American casserole based on Mexican tamales. In this version, the chili is mixed with corn and olives, poured into a cornmeal crust, topped with cheese and baked. A beanless, ground meat chili such as Rapid Fire Chili (page 20) is traditional, but you can also use chili with diced meat. You will need a 10-inch springform pan, or 7-cup or larger casserole.

ingredients

½ tsp. salt

¼ tsp. ground cumin

1 tsp. commercial chili powder

1 cup cornmeal

4 cups cooked chili

16-ounce can corn

5-ounce can olives, sliced

2 cups Cheddar or Monterey jack cheese, or a combination, grated

● Preheat the oven to 350°F. Spray a baking pan or casserole with non-stick spray.
● Bring 2 cups water to a boil in a large saucepan. Mix the salt, cumin, and chili powder and set aside. Mix the cornmeal and 1 cup cold water to form a thin, smooth paste. Slowly stir the cornmeal paste into the boiling water, stirring constantly. Reduce the heat to low, add the spice mix and continue stirring until the water is absorbed and the mixture is a thick mush. Remove from heat and let cool just a few minutes. Spread the cornmeal over the bottom and up the sides of the baking pan to form a crust. Let it cool while you prepare the filling.
● Mix the chili with the corn and olives, and reheat. The mixture should be thick, more like a paste than a stew. If the chili is soupy, mix 2 tablespoons cornmeal with 2 tablespoons cold water to form a

paste, then mix the paste into the chili.   ▲ *Tamale Pie*
Cook a few minutes until it is thick.

● Pour the chili into the crust. Sprinkle the
grated cheese over the top. Bake 30
minutes. Serve hot.

Chili Bean Sauce

ingredients

1 tsp. vegetable oil

1 medium onion, chopped

2 cloves garlic, minced

1 pound ground beef

2 cups beef stock

3 Tbsp. commercial chili powder

2 tsp. ground cumin

1–2 tsp. crushed red chile flakes

16-ounce can refried beans

about ½ tsp. salt

This mixture of refried beans and chili made with ground beef is a versatile and easy-to-make mixture. It makes a thick sauce that can be spooned over burgers and hot dogs. Or add corn chips, Cheddar cheese, and chopped onions, and eat it by the bowlful. The chili is moderately hot with 1 teaspoon chile flakes.

● Heat the oil in a skillet and sauté the onion and garlic 5 minutes. Remove the vegetables and set aside. Cook the ground beef in the skillet until browned. Drain off excess fat. Put the onion and beef in a large saucepan with the beef stock, stir well. Bring the mixture to a boil, reduce heat. Add the chili powder, cumin, and 1 teaspoon chile flakes.

● Simmer, adding water if needed, until the meat is falling apart, 45 minutes to 1 hour. The mixture should be a little soupy. Stir in the refried beans and cook 5 minutes. Taste, add salt and additional chile flakes if desired.

Chili Salad

ingredients

1 head iceberg lettuce, torn into pieces

3 cups chili, heated

½ cup green onions, chopped

8 ounces Cheddar cheese, grated

2¼-ounce can olives, sliced

2–3 tomatoes, cut into wedges

1 large or 2 small avocados, peeled and cut into wedges

2–3 cups corn chips

This is a salad that children will love – layers of chili, cheese and corn chips disguising the vegetables. A ground-meat chili with beans is preferred, but most chilis will do.

● Divide the lettuce among six serving plates. Spoon ½ cup of the hot chili over each. Sprinkle the green onions, cheese, and olives over the chili. Divide the tomato and avocado wedges among the plates, then top with corn chips.

▶ *Chili Salad*

106

CHILI ACCOMPANIMENTS

Even the most passionate chilihead wants something besides chili in his diet. There are certain dishes that always marry well with chili – beans, cornbread, cole slaw. Following are 18 recipes for foods to be served with chili – five kinds of beans, three kinds of cornbread, plus salads, breads, and dips.

Smoky Black Beans

MAKES 6 TO 8 SERVINGS

ingredients

2 cups black beans, picked over and soaked overnight

1 large onion, chopped

1½ tsp. smoked paprika

2 tsp. commercial chili powder

½ tsp. cayenne

1 large tomato, chopped

¼ cup fresh cilantro, chopped

2–3 tsp. salt

*S*moked paprika, a seasoning only recently available, adds a smoky flavor to these spicy black beans.

● Drain the beans, put them in a large saucepan with the chopped onion and cover with water. Bring the beans to a boil, reduce heat and simmer 1½ to 2 hours, adding water if needed.

● About 30 minutes before the beans are done, add the paprika, chili powder, and cayenne. When the beans are ready, add the tomato and cilantro and cook 2 minutes longer. Add salt, taste, and adjust seasonings.

Hot Black Beans

MAKES 6 TO 8 SERVINGS

ingredients

2 cups black beans, picked over and soaked overnight

1 large onion, chopped

2 Tbsp. chile flakes

1 tsp. ground cumin

3 cloves garlic, minced

2–3 tsp. salt

1 large tomato, seeded and diced

*C*hile flakes, hot red chiles that are dried and crushed, add plenty of heat to this bean dish.

● Drain the beans, put them in a large saucepan with the chopped onion and cover with water. Bring to a boil, reduce heat and simmer 1½ to 2 hours, adding water if needed.

● About 30 minutes before the beans are done, add the chile flakes, cumin, and garlic. When the beans are ready, add the salt and tomato. Taste and adjust seasonings.

▶ *Smoky Black Beans*

Pinto Beans and Ham Hocks

MAKES 6 TO 8 SERVINGS

ingredients

2 cups pinto beans, picked over and soaked overnight

1 large or 2 small smoked ham hocks

1 large onion, chopped

3 cloves garlic, minced

2 jalapeño chiles, unseeded and minced

½ cup green onions, finely chopped

¼ cup fresh cilantro, chopped

2–3 tsp. salt

*S*moked ham hocks lend their smoky flavor to these beans. The beans can be served as a side dish but make a substantial dish on their own. If you wish, chop the meat from the ham hocks and add it to the beans just before serving. The beans are hot, but the heat can be reduced by removing the veins and seeds from the jalapeños.

● Drain the beans, put in a pot with the ham hocks, onion, and garlic and add enough water to cover. Bring to a boil, reduce heat and simmer at least 1½ hours, adding water if needed. Add the jalapeños about 15 minutes before serving. When the beans are cooked, add the green onions, cilantro, and salt to taste.

Drunken Beans

MAKES 6 TO 8 SERVINGS

ingredients

2 cups pinto beans, picked over and soaked overnight

1 large onion, chopped

4 chiles de arbol, broken in half

12-ounce bottle dark Mexican beer

½ tsp. ground cumin

1 large tomato, peeled and chopped

2 Tbsp. fresh cilantro, chopped

about 1 Tbsp. salt

*S*immered in beer, these beans are pleasantly spicy with a hint of cumin.

● Put the beans, onion, and chiles in a large saucepan and add enough cold water to barely cover them. Add the beer and cumin. Bring to a boil, reduce heat and simmer at least 1½ hours. About 10 minutes before serving, add the tomato and cilantro. Add salt to taste.

▶ *Drunken Beans*

112

ingredients

1 or 2 ham hocks

2 bay leaves

2 Tbsp. vegetable oil

1 large onion, chopped

4 cloves garlic, minced

1 stalk celery, finely chopped

2 cups dry red beans, picked over and soaked overnight

2 carrots, peeled and finely chopped

8-ounce can tomato sauce

1 large or 2 small tomatoes, chopped (can be canned tomatoes)

2–3 jalapeño or serrano chiles

1 Tbsp. commercial chili powder

½ tsp. ground cumin

15-ounce can garbanzo beans

2–3 tsp. salt

Spicy Basque Beans

MAKES 8 TO 10 SIDE DISH SERVINGS

*O*ne of the ethnic groups that influenced the cuisine of the West Coast was Basque shepherds, who came to the inland valleys of California, Oregon, and Washington, as well as Idaho and Nevada in the 19th century. These beans might be served as a side dish at a Basque barbecue, but they can also be eaten as a light main dish. For a hot dish, leave the chile seeds and veins intact; remove them for a milder dish.

● Put the ham hocks and bay leaves in a large pot and add enough water to cover by 2 inches. Bring to a boil, reduce heat and simmer 30 minutes. While the ham hocks are simmering, cook the vegetables. Heat the oil in a large skillet and sauté the onion, garlic, and celery 5 minutes. Drain the beans.

● Add the sautéed vegetables and beans to the ham hocks. Add water to cover if needed. Bring to a boil, reduce heat and simmer another 30 minutes. Remove the ham hocks from the beans and let them cool about 15 minutes. Meanwhile, add the remaining ingredients, except the garbanzo beans and salt, to the beans.

● When the ham hocks are cool enough to handle, cut the meat and fat from the bones. Discard the fat and bones. Shred the meat and add it to the beans.

● Cook the beans until they are tender, adding water if needed, a total of about 1½ hours. Add the garbanzo beans. Taste, add salt, and adjust seasonings. Cook about 10 minutes longer.

Mexican Corn Muffins

MAKES 16 TO 20 MUFFINS

*S*tudded with corn and jalapeño chiles and flavored with Cheddar cheese, these muffins complement any chili.

● Preheat the oven to 375°F. Lightly grease or spray muffin tins. Combine the cornmeal, flour, salt, baking powder and soda, and sugar in a large bowl.

● In a small bowl, lightly beat the eggs with a fork. Mix the melted butter and buttermilk, and pour into the eggs. Stir in the corn and chiles. Pour the liquids into the dry ingredients and beat by hand until the batter is mixed. Stir in the cheese. Pour the batter into the muffin tins, filling them to just below the rim. Bake 25 to 30 minutes, until golden.

ingredients

1½ cups cornmeal

½ cup all-purpose flour

1 tsp. salt

2 tsp. baking powder

1 tsp. baking soda

1 Tbsp. sugar

3 eggs

½ cup melted butter

1 cup buttermilk

15-ounce can cream-style corn

6 jalapeño chiles, seeded and chopped

2 cups Cheddar cheese, grated

Skillet Cornbread with Bacon and Jalapeños

MAKES 8 SERVINGS

ingredients

4 strips bacon

2¼ cups cornmeal

¾ cup all-purpose flour

1½ tsp. salt

1 Tbsp. baking powder

2 Tbsp. sugar

2 eggs, lightly beaten

2 cups milk

½ cup melted butter, or butter and bacon fat

4 jalapeño chiles, seeded and minced

With a dense texture and minimal sugar, this is a traditional cornbread, but for the addition of jalapeño chiles. It is baked in a sizzling-hot skillet, and seasoned with bacon fat and bits of fried bacon, much like old-fashioned cracklin' cornbread. A heavy, 9-inch or 10-inch cast-iron skillet is required.

● Preheat the oven to 425°F. Fry the bacon until crisp in a cast-iron skillet. Remove the bacon and drain on paper towels. When the bacon is cool enough to handle, crumble it. Save about 1 tablespoon bacon fat for the pan. Discard the rest, or combine with melted butter to make ½ cup fat. Combine the dry ingredients.

● Brush bacon fat around the bottom and up the sides of the skillet so it is completely oiled. Put the skillet in the oven to heat.

● In a separate bowl, lightly beat the eggs with a fork. Combine the milk and melted butter or butter/bacon fat combination, then add to the eggs. Stir in the chiles. Pour the liquids into the dry ingredients and stir by hand until the batter is well-mixed. Stir in the bacon crumbles.

● The skillet should be very hot and the bacon fat just short of smoking. Carefully pour the batter into the skillet. It will sizzle as it hits the fat. Bake until the cornbread is golden brown, 35 to 40 minutes. Let cool slightly, then cut into wedges. Serve warm.

Light, Sweet Cornbread

MAKES 9 SERVINGS

ingredients

1¾ cups all-purpose flour

1¼ cups cornmeal

½ cup sugar

2 tsp. baking powder

1 tsp. baking soda

1 tsp. salt

2 eggs

1½ cups buttermilk

½ cup melted butter

Most chili aficionados prefer a dense cornbread with no sweetening and a low proportion of flour. This recipe is for those who like a light, sweet cornbread.

● Preheat the oven to 350°F. Spray or lightly butter an 8-by-8-inch baking pan. Mix the dry ingredients in a large bowl.

● In a small bowl, lightly beat the eggs with a fork. Stir in the buttermilk, then the melted butter. Pour the liquids into the dry ingredients and beat the batter by hand until well-blended.

● Pour the batter into the baking pan. Bake until the cornbread is golden brown, 35 to 40 minutes. Cool slightly before cutting into nine squares.

Chile Con Queso

MAKES 12 TO 16 APPETIZER SERVINGS

ingredients

2 Tbsp. butter

2–3 jalapeño chiles, minced

1 clove garlic, minced

1 medium tomato, seeded and chopped

3 green onions, minced

8 ounces Cheddar cheese, grated

8 ounces Monterey jack cheese, grated

Chile con queso is a sort of Southwestern fondue – melted cheese with chiles, onions, garlic, and tomatoes. It is a terrific dip for chips, crackers, or crudités, or can be a main dish fondue, served with chunks of bread. It can be kept warm by setting the pot over a candle or on a warming tray. For a mild dip, remove the seeds and veins from the jalapeños.

● Preheat the oven to 350°F. Heat the butter in a skillet and sauté the chiles, garlic, tomatoes, and green onions for 5 minutes. Continue cooking, if needed, until the liquids have evaporated.

● Stir the vegetables into the grated cheese in an ovenproof serving dish. Bake until the cheese is bubbling, about 12 minutes. Serve immediately.

▶ *Chile Con Queso*

118

Navajo Fry Bread

ingredients

2 cups all-purpose flour

1½ tsp. baking powder

¾ tsp. salt

¼ cup non-fat dry milk

¾ cup water

vegetable oil or lard for frying

Golden, puffy Navajo Fry Bread is a tradition of the American Southwest. It goes well with any chili, but especially with green chile stews.

● Combine the dry ingredients together. Add the water and knead the dough until soft. Divide the dough into six equal pieces. Shape each piece into a round, then flatten each round to a thickness of ¼–½ inch. Poke a small hole in the center of each.

● Pour oil or melt lard in a large skillet or Dutch oven to a depth of 1 inch and heat to 375°F. Carefully drop one or two rounds of dough into the hot oil, keeping the rounds separated. Fry, turning once, until both sides are golden and puffy, about 1 minute a side. Remove, let drain for a few seconds. Repeat until all the rounds are fried. Serve hot.

Salsa Fresca

ingredients

1½–2 cups chopped tomatoes

½ medium red onion, finely chopped

2 jalapeño chiles, partly seeded, minced

1 clove garlic, minced

3–4 Tbsp. fresh cilantro, chopped

2 Tbsp. fresh lime juice

1–2 Tbsp. olive oil

dash salt

Few extras accompany chili as well as salsa and tortilla chips. Here is a recipe for a moderately hot fresh salsa that should be made no more than a few hours before it is to be eaten. The ingredients, especially the tomatoes, should be chopped by hand. A food processor will turn the tomatoes into pink mush. It's important that the tomatoes are ripe, or they will add little flavor to the salsa.

● Combine all the ingredients together in a bowl. Let sit at least 30 minutes at room temperature before serving.

▶ *Navajo Fry Bread*

Avocado Salsa

MAKES ABOUT 2½ CUPS

ingredients

3 avocados, preferably Haas, diced

1 medium or 2 Roma tomatoes, diced

½ medium red onion, finely chopped

2 jalapeño chiles, minced

3 Tbsp. fresh lime juice

1 Tbsp. olive oil

1 Tbsp. fresh cilantro, chopped

dash salt and black pepper

A*vocado salsa is similar to guacamole, but the avocado is cubed rather than mashed, and is mixed with minced chiles. Use it as a dip for chips or a topping for chili. If your avocados are slightly short of being perfectly ripe, add a little bottled avocado oil to improve the flavor of the salsa. If you mix the other ingredients in advance, don't dice the avocados until just before serving. Remove the seeds and veins from the jalapeño chiles for a milder salsa.*

● Combine all the ingredients together in a bowl.

Karen's Jalapeño Breadsticks

Karen Nitkin was experimenting with no-fat recipes for her bread machine when she came across an odd one that used bananas instead of fat to make spicy breadsticks. The bananas didn't appeal to her, but the combination of garlic, jalapeño chiles, and Parmesan cheese did, so she compromised a bit on the fat and came up with these. Extra-long and chewy, they are an excellent accompaniment to chili.

ingredients

1½ cups bread flour
¾ cup whole wheat flour
½ tsp. salt
¼ cup yellow cornmeal
2 cloves garlic, minced
1 egg white
½ cup Parmesan cheese
2 jalapeño chiles, minced
⅔ cup water
¼ cup vegetable oil
1½ tsp. yeast

FOR BREAD MACHINES:

● Combine the ingredients and place in the bread machine. Program the machine for dough. Remove the kneaded dough from the bread machine and let sit in an oiled bowl for 20 minutes. Preheat the oven to 350°F. Cut the dough into nine pieces. Roll each piece into a long stick on an unfloured surface. Bake for 20 minutes, until the sticks brown slightly. Let cool and serve.

BY HAND:

● Heat the water to between 105 and 115°F. Add a pinch of flour and the yeast. Let sit until the mixture develops a foamy head, about 10 minutes.

● While the yeast is proofing, combine all the other ingredients, except the flours. Gradually stir in about half the flour. Turn the dough onto a lightly floured surface and knead in the remaining flour. Total kneading time should be 8 to 10 minutes. Place the dough in an oiled bowl, cover with a clean towel, and put in a warm place to rise for about 1½ hours. Punch down the dough, then let sit about 20 minutes. Preheat the oven to 350°F. Cut the dough into nine pieces. Roll each piece into a long stick on an unfloured surface. Bake for 20 minutes, until the sticks brown slightly. Let cool and serve.

◀ *Avocado Salsa*

Cilantro Chili Dip

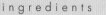

This cheesy layered dip should be served hot with tortilla chips and eaten quickly before the melted cheese hardens. Use a ground-meat chili, with or without beans.

● Preheat the oven to 375°F. With a wooden spoon, stir the cilantro and chile into the cream cheese. Spread the cream cheese over the bottom of a soufflé dish or small glass pie plate. Spread the chili over the cream cheese. Sprinkle the green onions over the chili, and sprinkle the cheese over the top. Bake until the cheese is bubbly, about 12 minutes.

3 Tbsp. fresh cilantro, chopped

1 jalapeño chile, seeded and minced

8 ounces cream cheese, softened

1 cup chili, heated

3 green onions, chopped

6 ounces Monterey jack cheese, grated

Hot Bean Dip

This easy party dip is made with black beans, leftover chili, and fresh or bottled salsa of your choice. Use California Five Way Chili (page 79), Beef and Chorizo Chili (page 36), or other chili made with ground meat and no beans. You can use canned beans, but freshly cooked dried beans provide a better flavor and texture. The dip should be served hot with chips.

● Put all the ingredients in a blender or food processor. Purée in short bursts, using the pulse button, until the mixture is coarsely chopped, not smooth. Reheat the dip, taste, and adjust seasonings.

3 cups cooked black beans

1 cup leftover chili, heated

1 cup salsa

1 tsp. ground cumin

salt to taste

▶ *Tomato-cucumber Salad with Spicy Vinaigrette*

Tomato-cucumber Salad with Spicy Vinaigrette

MAKES 4 SERVINGS

*M*ake this cooling salad several hours before serving so the vegetables absorb the flavors of the vinaigrette.

● Combine the olive oil, lime juice, vinegar, garlic, cilantro, honey, hot pepper sauce, salt and pepper in a blender or food processor. Purée.

● Combine the tomatoes, cucumber, and red onion. Toss with the dressing.

ingredients

⅓ cup olive oil

2 Tbsp. fresh lime juice

1 Tbsp. red wine vinegar

1 clove garlic, coarsely chopped

⅓ cup whole cilantro leaves

1 tsp. honey

few drops hot pepper sauce

dash salt

dash black pepper

4 beefsteak tomatoes, sliced

½ cucumber, peeled and thinly sliced

6 thin slices red onion, separated into rings

Southwestern Corn Salad with Rajas

*T*his corn salad is spicy but not hot and can be used as a relish with grilled meats. It is made with rajas, *strips of roasted chile and red bell pepper. When possible, use fresh corn just cut from the cob, but frozen corn is acceptable. The salad is best when made several hours in advance so the flavors have a chance to blend, but not so long that it loses its crunch. If the salad is made in advance, the avocado should be cut and added just before serving.*

ingredients

¼ cup olive oil

3 Tbsp. fresh lime juice

2 Tbsp. fresh cilantro, finely chopped

½ tsp. ground cumin

1 clove garlic, minced

dash salt

dash pepper

1 poblano chile

1 sweet red bell pepper

3 cups corn, fresh or frozen

½ green bell pepper, cut into ¼-inch dice

2 medium tomatoes, seeded and chopped

⅓ medium red onion, finely chopped

1 large avocado, peeled and diced

● Combine the olive oil, lime juice, cilantro, cumin, garlic, salt, and pepper, and shake well to make dressing. Set aside.

● Roast the chile and red bell pepper under the broiler, turning often, until all sides are charred, about 10 minutes. Remove and place in a paper bag or covered bowl. Let steam for at least 10 minutes.

● While the chile and pepper are cooling, cook the corn. Put the corn in a small pan with about ½ cup water. Bring to a boil and cook 5 minutes. Drain the corn and let it cool.

● Remove the chile and pepper from the bag or bowl. Peel and discard the blackened skin, stems, and seeds. Cut the chile and pepper into narrow strips.

● To make the salad, combine the corn, chile and pepper strips, and remaining ingredients. Toss with the dressing. Taste and adjust seasonings.

Cole Slaw

Cole slaw is a traditional accompaniment to chili, its tangy coolness offsetting the chili's bite. For a more colorful slaw, substitute red cabbage for half the green cabbage. For variety, add dill or caraway seeds to the dressing. When possible, make the dressing a few hours in advance to allow the flavors to blend, then mix with the cabbage about 30 minutes before serving.

● Mix the cabbage and carrots in a large bowl. Combine the remaining ingredients and whisk to make a smooth dressing. Toss with the cabbage.

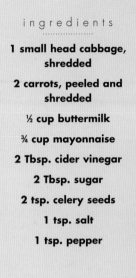

ingredients

1 small head cabbage, shredded

2 carrots, peeled and shredded

½ cup buttermilk

¾ cup mayonnaise

2 Tbsp. cider vinegar

2 Tbsp. sugar

2 tsp. celery seeds

1 tsp. salt

1 tsp. pepper

Index